Table of Contents

©www.CoreCommonStandards.com

Common Core State Standards

Fourth Grade Workbook
STUDENT EDITION

Grade 4

- **Math Standards**
- **English Standards**

Worksheets that teach every Common Core Standard!

Name: _____

iPod

Directions: Read the passage below about an iPod. Answer the questions about the text. Cite examples from the text to support your answers.

Trent had asked for only one thing for his birthday...a new iPod. His older brother, Trey, already had one and was very particular about who got to use it, and for how long. Trent couldn't wait to have his very own and decide who could borrow it and when.

He started leaving clues around the house a full month before his birthday. He cut out pictures from ad papers, left sticky-notes with drawings of iPods on his mom's vanity mirror, and placed a Polaroid picture in his dad's truck of himself using Trey's iPod. Trent wasn't so sure his hints would be enough, so to further guarantee his parent's purchase of the gift, he emptied the trash without being asked, kept his room clean, and didn't fight once with Trey. A new iPod was as good as his.

The morning of his birthday, Trent woke up and was super excited! He had to wait all day for his party to begin and the anticipation was making him light-headed. As the time for the party arrived, Trent was ready to burst. He could barely contain his enthusiasm. Right after the cake, which Trent ate so fast he couldn't recall the flavor, he began opening presents. Fifteen gifts, and not one was an iPod. Beginning to feel queasy and very confused, Trent felt a feeling of despair come over him.

In a daze, he rose to head into the kitchen to retrieve a soda bottle from the refrigerator as his mom had instructed him to do. Trent opened the door slowly and, staring into the bright light of the cold fridge, on the top shelf he saw a bright, white, shiny box with a little, white apple on it and a tiny, red bow.   Trent just grinned.

Answer these questions about the text.

1. How does Trent feel during most of this story? Cite evidence.

He feels excited and anxuis because he keeps putting stickers pictures and sticky notes to his parents about the Ipod.

2. How do you think Trent felt after opening the presents and seeing no iPod? Why?

I think he felt sad because he spent so much time bieng good and didn't get an ipod.

3. Why does Trent leave hints around the house?

Trent leaves hints because he wants an ipod for his birthday

Name: _____

Major General

Directions: Read the passage below about Major General. Answer the questions about the text. Cite examples from the text to support your answers.

Sean had practiced for this night for three months. Several times a week, he would sing in front of the camera on his mom's computer and watch the video to see what parts needed improvement. Sean had decided to sing a song from Pirates of Penzance, an opera, for the school's talent show. The opera is actually a funny story and the song Sean chose was fun to sing; *I Am the Very Model of a Modern Major General*. But, it was hard. The song was fast-paced with lots of big, mathematical, historical, and scientific words. Words like animalculous, Aristophanes, commissariat, and binomial theorem especially tripped up his tongue.

As Sean waited to walk onto the stage, all decked out in the costume his mom made and the large-plumed hat which he had bought at Disney World, he was a little nervous, but he felt confident. The curtain slowly rose after the Master-of-Ceremonies introduced Sean. He marched out, as Generals tend to do, straight and stiff holding a cane and the microphone. He turned to face the audience, and stood, staring. Sean was singing *a cappella*...without music, so he wasn't waiting for a cue. The room was packed and Sean began to sweat. His hands became clammy. His heart started to pound. He was short of breath and felt an intense urge to march right back, stage left.

But, suddenly, a surge of courage overwhelmed Sean when he looked beyond the crowd and saw his mom standing in the back, giving him a thumbs-up. Immediately he belted out, in a loud, strong voice heard in the hallway...I am the very model of a modern major general!

Answer these questions about the text.

1. Where does this story take place? What evidence tells you that?

The story takes place in the School auditorium and the boys bedroom. The school auditorium because it says he performed there and the boys bedroom because he practiced there.

2. How does Sean feel when he is standing on the stage? How do you know?

Sean felt nervous and sweaty on the stage. It said in the story.

3. Why do you think Sean chose a tough song to sing? What would you choose?

Sean chose a hard song because he has courage and is good at singing. I would chose an easy song.

Standard: Reading I Literature I RL.4.1

©http://CoreCommonStandards.com

Name: _____

Theme

The theme is the underlying message of a piece of text. It can be a lesson or moral.
Authors sometimes tell the theme at the end of a story.
Most times, the theme is an inference. You need to find some clues. Look for words, phrases, or
sentences that recur in the text. What feeling do you get from the text?

Directions: Choose a story, drama, or poem to read and determine a theme by the details of the text.
Summarize the text and write the theme.

Story: _____ **Genre:**_____

Who are the characters?

_____

What is the setting?

_____

What problems are the characters experiencing?

_____

_____

How do the characters deal with the problems?

_____

_____

What feelings do you get from this story?

_____

_____

What might be the theme of this story?

_____

_____

Standard: Reading I Literature I RL.4.2

Name: _____

Theme

The theme is the underlying message of a piece of text. It can be a lesson or moral. Authors sometimes tell the theme at the end of a story. Most times, the theme is an inference. You need to find some clues. Look for words, phrases, or sentences that recur in the text. What feeling do you get from the text?

Directions: Determine the themes of each of the stories below. If you haven't yet read the story, now's a good time.

Charlotte's Web	Talkin' About Bessie	To Market, To Market
_____ _____ _____ _____	_____ _____ _____ _____	_____ _____ _____ _____
The Keeping Quilt	Arthur's Eyes	Because of Winn Dixie
_____ _____ _____ _____	_____ _____ _____ _____	_____ _____ _____ _____

Name: _____

Theme

The theme is the underlying message of a piece of text. It can be a lesson or moral. Authors sometimes tell the theme at the end of a story. Most times, the theme is an inference. You need to find some clues. Look for words, phrases, or sentences that recur in the text. What feeling do you get from the text?

Directions: Determine the themes of each of the stories below. If you haven't yet read the story, now's a good time.

Charlie and the Chocolate Factory	Holes	Mr. Popper's Penguins
_____	_____	_____
Sarah, Plain and Tall	James and the Giant Peach	The Tale of Despereaux
_____	_____	_____

Name: _____

Character

Directions: Choose a story, drama, or poem to read and describe one character from the text. Use details from the text to support your thoughts.

Story: _____ **Genre:** _____

Character name: _____

Describe what the character looks like.

_____

_____

What is the character's problem?

_____

_____

How does the character feel at the beginning, middle, and end of the story?

_____

_____

_____

Describe the actions the character takes to solve his or her problem.

_____

_____

_____

Do you agree with what the character does? Why or why not?

_____

_____

_____

Do you feel a connection to the character? Why or why not?

_____

_____

_____

Standard: Reading I Literature I RL.4.3

Name: _____

Setting

Directions: Choose a story, drama, or poem to read and describe one setting from the text. Use details from the text to support your thoughts.

Story: _____ **Genre:** _____

Setting: _____

Describe the setting.

where:_____

_____

when:_____

_____

Why does this setting work for the text you read?

_____

_____

What are some words or thoughts the characters or narrator use that give you an idea of the setting?

_____

_____

_____

How would the story change if the setting changed?

_____

_____

_____

Do you feel a connection to the setting? Why or why not?

_____

_____

_____

Standard: Reading I Literature I RL.4.3

Name: _____

Vocabulary with the Frayer Model

Directions: Read *Charlie and the Chocolate Factory*.
Choose one of the story's vocabulary words from the box
at the bottom of the page and complete the Frayer Model below.

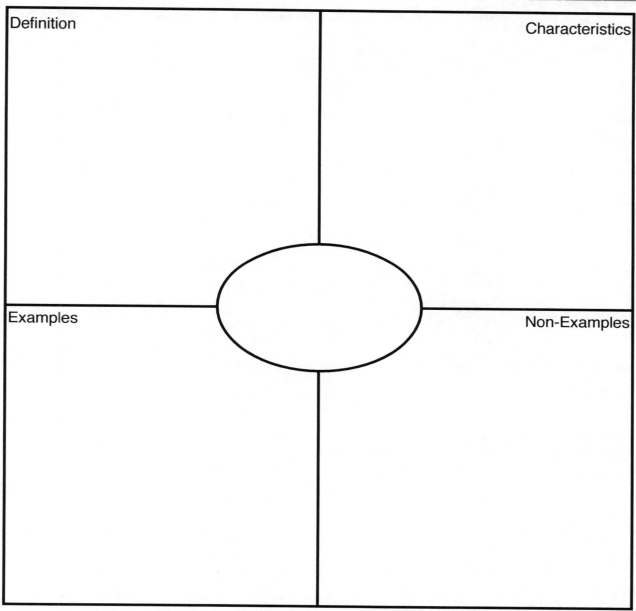

Definition

Characteristics

Examples

Non-Examples

colossal   stammer   anxious   hooligans
ravenously   pandemonium   corridor
froth   frump   precipice

Name: _____

Mythological Vocabulary

Directions: The following words are from *The Odyssey* written by Homer. Use Greek Mythology resources, or read *The Odyssey*, to determine the original mythological meanings of the words. Use a dictionary to write the modern definition of each.

Word or Phrase	Modern Definition	Mythological Definition
Example: Cornucopia	a great abundance; overflowing supply	a horn containing food, drink, etc., in endless supply, said to have been a horn of the goat Amalthaea.
1. Nemesis		
2. Olympic		
3. Achilles' Heel		
4. Labyrinth		
5. Herculean		
6. Atlas		
7. Phoenix		

Name: _____

Contrasting Prose and Poetry

Prose is the writing we see and use most often. It's purpose is to share information or entertain. Poetry's purpose is the use of the language as music.

Directions: Read the familiar poem *Three Blind Mice*, below. Think about how prose is constructed and rewrite the poem in a prose form. Use new vocabulary to create your prose.

POEM

Three blind mice.
Three blind mice.

See how they run,
See how they run.

They all went after the farmer's wife,
Who cut off their tale with a carving knife.

Have you ever seen such a sight in your life
As there blind mice?

PROSE

_____

_____

_____

_____

_____

_____

_____

_____

How do the two versions differ?

In what ways are they the same?

Name: _____

Drama, Poetry, & Prose

Read each description. Then decide what each one is best describing. Some might have more than one answer. Put a checkmark in the drama, poetry, and/or prose column for each description that fits it.

#	DESCRIPTION	DRAMA	POETRY	PROSE
1	purpose is to inform, entertain, express, or persuade			
2	written using paragraphs			
3	doesn't always follow punctuation and grammar rules			
4	purpose is to entertain or express opinions			
5	may contain dialogue			
6	can take the form of a biography, novel, essay, short story, fable, or article			
7	uses words to create images			
8	uses rhyme, alliteration, onomatopoeia			
9	usually performed			
10	may have staging directions, list of characters, and be written in script form			
11	can take the form of a haiku, acrostic, ballad, shape, or narrative			
12	can be written as a skit, play, opera, musical, or monologue			
13	written in lines and stanzas			

Which type of writing is your favorite? Why?

_____

_____

_____

Name: _____

Points of View

Directions: Read *Hey, Little Ant,* by Phillip M. Hoose. Compare and contrast the points-of-view of each character.

The Boy's point-of-view about squishing the Ant.

_____

_____

What are some things the boy says in the story that support his point-of-view?

_____

_____

_____

_____

The Ant's point-of-view about being squished by the Boy.

_____

_____

What are some things the ant says in the story that support his point-of-view?

_____

_____

_____

_____

Name: _____

First or Third Person?

Directions: Read the sentences below. Mark (✔) if the sentence is told in first person or third person.

The **first person narrative** is when a character inside the story is the one telling the story. This allows the reader to know what a character is thinking. Common pronouns used in a first person narrative are 'I' and 'we.'

The **third person narrative** is when someone outside the story is telling the story. They narrate the story.

		First Person	Third Person
1	I was late for school this morning.		
2	John and Frank played football today.		
3	Dan dropped his lollipop on the floor.		
4	We are going to the circus with Pat.		
5	I really want a new puppy for a pet.		
6	Louisa plays the trumpet really well.		
7	Dad went for a walk with mom last night.		
8	She is not afraid of spiders like Rick.		
9	Beatrice gave a birthday present to me.		
10	Barney's group read a book together.		

Name: _____

Illustration Connection

Directions: Read the story *The Secret Garden* by Frances H. Brunett.
Look at the pictures illustrated by Graham Rust throughout the book.
Choose 2 pictures to copy or recreate and find the passage in the text that the
picture illustrates. Write the description that explicitly connects with the picture.
Explain the connection.

The Secret Garden

Illustration	Text evidence of illustration connection.
	Student explanation of the connection.

Illustration	Text evidence of illustration connection.
	Student explanation of the connection.

Standard: Reading I Literature I RL.4.7

Level: Fourth Grade

Name: _____

The BFG

Directions: Read *The BFG* and *The BFG: a Set of Plays*, by Roald Dahl. Compare and contrast the two versions, possibly acting out one of the plays. Make connections between the two versions. Compare where each version reflects specific descriptions and directions in the text.

The BFG

The BFG:
A Set of
Plays

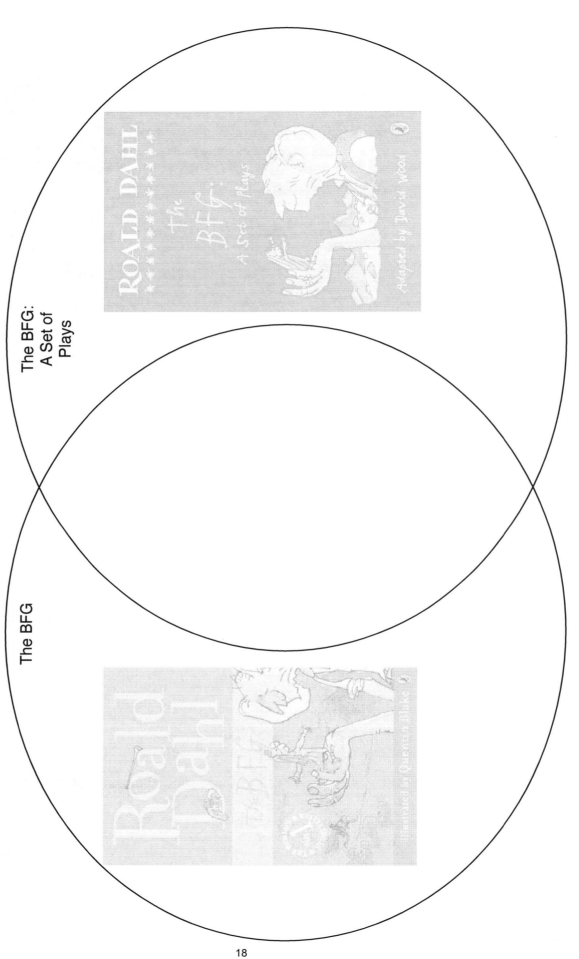

18

Standard: Reading I Literature I RL.4.7

Name: _____

After acting out a scene from The BFG: A Set of Plays, write the direction and character dialogue and how it was represented in action.

Scene _____

Write a part of the scene's text.

_____

_____

_____

_____

How was the direction and description represented in action?

_____

_____

_____

_____

19

Standard: Reading l Literature l RL.4.7

Name: _____

Good vs Evil

Directions: Read stories where the theme of good vs evil is prevalent. Some stories that follow this theme are *Matilda* (Roald Dahl), *Harry Potter* (J. K. Rowling), *The Wizard of Oz* (Frank L. Baum), *Lord of the Flies* (William Golding), and *A Wrinkle in Time* (Madeleine L'Engle).

Story 1 _____ **Author**	**Story 2** _____ **Author**
_____ **Setting**	_____ **Setting**
Main Character(s) Write if the character is good or evil, and why. (citing text evidence)	**Main Character(s)** Write if the character is good or evil, and why. (citing text evidence)
Does Good Prevail? How?	**Does Good Prevail? How?**

©http://CoreCommonStandards.com

Name: _____

Growing Up

Directions: Read stories where the theme of growing up is prevalent. Some stories that follow this theme are *Charley Skedaddle* (Patricia Beatty), *The Moon Bridge* (Marcia Savin), *Cosmic* (Frank C. Boyce), and *Otherwise Known as Sheila the Great* by Judy Blume.

_____
Story 1

_____
Author

_____
Setting

Main Character(s)
What are the events the main character faces in the story?

_____
_____
_____
_____
_____
_____
_____
_____
_____
_____

How are the character's problems resolved?

_____
_____

_____
Story 2

_____
Author

_____
Setting

Main Character(s)
What are the events the main character faces in the story?

_____
_____
_____
_____
_____
_____
_____
_____
_____
_____

How are the character's problems resolved?

_____
_____

Level: Fourth Grade   Name: _____

What I Am Reading

Directions: Keep track of the stories you read this year in Fourth Grade. When you finish a book, write the title and the date you completed the book. Would you recommend the book? Why or why not?

Date	Book Title	Recommend?

Standard: Reading I Literature I RL.4.10   ©http://CoreCommonStandards.com

22

Level: Fourth Grade

Name: _____

What Are They Reading?

Directions: Keep track of the stories your students can read this year at grade level. Write the date each genre was read successfully.

Name	non-fiction story	realistic fiction story	fantasy story	informational story	poetry

Standard: Reading I Literature I RL.4.10

Name: _____

Dr. William Beaumont

Directions: Read the passage below about Dr. William Beaumont. Answer the question about the text.

William Beaumont is known for his experiments on the digestive system and the information learned from those experiments. He was born in Lebanon, Connecticut on November 21, 1785. On September 13, 1812, when he was 26, William went into the army as a surgeon's mate to serve during the War of 1812. After the war, Beaumont left the army and began private practice in June, 1815, in Plattsburgh, NY. There he met Deborah Green Platt. In December, 1819, William went back to the army as a post surgeon. He was sent to Fort Mackinac in Lake Huron. The hospital was in a storehouse. They had little supplies, and no thermometer.

On June 6, 1822, Alexis St. Martin was shot by an accidental discharge of a shotgun in the upper left of his abdomen. St. Martin was brought to Dr. Beaumont where he found the man's latest meal gushing out of the wound. Beaumont cleaned the hole, but could not keep the contents of his stomach from falling out unless it was bandaged.

On August 1, 1825, Beaumont began to experiment on St. Martin's stomach. Those experiments included tying string to a piece of food and lowering it into St. Martin's stomach. After a few hours, Beaumont would take it out to see the extent of digestion. In one experiment, the food was removed after five hours for Alexis had a severe stomachache. The next day, St. Martin still had stomach problems, and Beaumont helped. Six days later, St. Martin didn't eat for 17 hours (on Doctor's orders!) so Beaumont could find the temperature of the stomach, which was 100 degrees. When Dr. Beaumont observed St. Martin on dry days, he saw that the temperature of the stomach increased, and vice versa on humid days. Beaumont would have St. Martin eat a meal, and then would later take out samples of the food and put them in separate vials of water, and gastric juice. He observed that cold stomach acid does nothing, so digestion needs heat. He also learned that when Alexis showed anger, it slowed the digestion process.

In April, 1833, Beaumont published his work and findings in a book called: *Experiments and observations on the gastric juice and the physiology of digestion.* A month or so later Alexis left for Canada, and Beaumont went into private medical practice. Dr. William Beaumont kept up the private practice in St. Louis. In March, 1853, Beaumont was leaving a patient when he slipped on the icy steps and hit his head. He died a month later on April 25, and was buried in Bellefontaine Cemetery in St. Louis.

Answer

Explain what Dr. Beaumont is known for. What are some of his most important findings?

Dr. Beaumont was known for
his digestive system expiraments. experiments.
Some of his most finding were
anger made digestive system digest
slower and heat made it digest
faster,

Name: _____

Environment

Directions: Read the passage below about the environment. Answer the questions about the text. Cite examples from the text to support your answers.

People talk a lot about the environment these days. Our environment is everything around us; natural, man-made, cultural, and social. But what most people are referring to when they speak of the environment are the factors that impact the survival of living things and their needs.

Living organisms require certain things to remain living, to prosper and propagate, and give back to the environment. Because all living things are tied together through the food chain, affecting one member of our animal or plant world ultimately affects all living things. For example, some farmers use pesticides (insecticides, herbicides, and fungicides) to protect crops.   Small amounts of these pesticides travel through the air landing in soils. The pesticides can enter small insects, such as grasshoppers. Mice and shrews will eat many grasshoppers, thus ingesting larger amounts of the chemicals. Larger animals, such as birds, will eat many mice, and the pattern continues.

Oceans and other waterways can become polluted when oil and waste is deposited into streams and rivers. Aquatic animals, many of which are eaten by people, swim in and ingest these pollutants. If we continue to pollute our water, we not only risk many species' existence, but also the quality and quantity of our own drinking water.

It is everyone's responsibility to care for our environment. It is easy, and you can help. You can recycle, stop littering, use fewer plastic products, and use natural products and fewer chemicals. Recognize that it is your job. It's your Earth!

Answer these questions about the text.

1. How does one act affect the larger environment? Cite evidence.

   Because if a farmer put chemicals on his plants the grasshopper will eat that and get the chemical inside it and whatever eats it gets the diseas.

2. Discuss a way people can positively affect the environment.

   You can stop littering and recycle.

3. Why is the topic of our environment so important?

   Because if the environment wasn't working right we wond no be alive.

Name: _____

The Poison Dart Frog

Directions: Read the passage below about poison dart frogs. What is the main idea of the text? Determine the key details and how they support the main idea. Summarize the text.

Poison dart frogs wear some of the most brilliant and beautiful colors on Earth. Depending on their habitats, which are from the tropical forests of Costa Rica to Brazil, their coloring can be yellow, gold, copper, red, green, blue, or black. Their designs and colors scare off predators.

You may have seen monkeys carrying their children on their backs. Well, some of these frogs show some of these parenting habits, including carrying both eggs and tadpoles on their backs.

These frogs are some of the most toxic animals on Earth. The two-inch-long Golden Poison Dart Frog has enough venom to kill 10 grown men. Indigenous people of Colombia have used its powerful venom for centuries to tip their blowgun darts when hunting.

Scientists are not sure why these poison dart frogs are so poisonous, but it is possible they take in plant poisons which are carried by their prey, including ants, termites and beetles. Poison dart frogs raised in captivity and isolated from insects in their native habitat never develop venom.

The medical research community has been exploring ways to use poison dart frog venom in medicine. Scientists have already used their venom to create a painkiller medicine.

What is the main idea of this passage? _____

Key Detail _____

_____

How it supports the main idea.

_____

_____

_____

_____

Key Detail _____

_____

How it supports the main idea.

_____

_____

_____

_____

Key Detail _____

_____

How it supports the main idea.

_____

_____

_____

_____

Key Detail _____

_____

How it supports the main idea.

_____

_____

_____

_____

Standard: Reading I Informational Text I RI.4.2   ©http://CoreCommonStandards.com
Text By: http://animals.nationalgeographic.com

The Poison Dart Frog

Directions: Read the passage above about poison dart frogs. Summarize the text below.

_____
_____
_____
_____
_____
_____
_____
_____
_____
_____
_____
_____
_____
_____
_____
_____
_____
_____
_____
_____
_____
_____
_____
_____
_____
_____
_____

Standard: Reading I Informational Text I RI.4.2
Text By: http://animals.nationalgeographic.com

Name: _____

Lemurs

Directions: Read the passage below about lemurs. What is the main idea of the text? Determine the key details and how they support the main idea. Summarize the text.

Lemurs are primates known as prosimians, which means pre-primates or before monkeys. They are native to Madagascar, an island country located in the Indian Ocean off the southeastern coast of Africa. Scientist believe there are five families of lemurs containing 30 living species.   Some species are now extinct.

Most lemurs live in trees spending most of their time at the top of the rainforest canopy or in the midlevel sections. The ring-tailed lemur, however, spends most of its time on the ground. Many of the lemurs are diurnal, which means they are awake during the day and asleep at night. The smaller lemurs, such as the mouse and dwarf lemurs, are nocturnal, being active in the dark when it is safer.

Lemurs differ from other primates in that they do not have a prehensile tail, which means they cannot hang by their tales like monkeys do. What lemurs do have is a keen sense of smell and big eyes with good vision as well as opposable thumbs.

Some of the many species of lemurs are endangered and may soon be on the endangered list. There are "adopt-a-lemur" organizations and many groups that hope to bring awareness to the Lemur's plight so that these primates may continue to of flourish on our earth.

What is the mail idea of this passage?_____

Key Detail_____	Key Detail_____
_____	_____
How it supports the main idea.	How it supports the main idea.
Key Detail_____	Key Detail_____
_____	_____
How it supports the main idea.	How it supports the main idea.

©http://CoreCommonStandards.com

Name: _____

Lemurs

Directions: Read the passage above about lemurs. Summarize the text below.

Name: _____

Notes on a Bookmark

Directions: With a partner, read a historical text. Take notes on the bookmarks below, one for each partner. After reading and collecting important information, compare your notes. Retell the text passage using your bookmark notes.

Historical Text Selection_____

Name: _____

Title: _____

What?

_____

_____

_____

_____

When?

_____

Where?

_____

Why?

_____

_____

_____

Name: _____

Title: _____

What?

_____

_____

_____

_____

When?

_____

Where?

_____

Why?

_____

_____

_____

Standard: Reading I Informational Text I RI.4.3
Graphics (c) ScrappinDoodles

Level: Fourth Grade   Name: _____

Scientific Time Line

Directions: With a partner, read a text about a scientific discovery. Complete the time line with facts from the text. Summarize the text.

Scientific Discovery _____   **Scientist(s)** _____

Text _____   **Author(s)** _____

Beginning

□ → □ → □ → □

Ending

□ → □ → □ → □

31

Standard: Reading I Informational Text I RI.4.3   ©http://CoreCommonStandards.com

Name: _____

Word Meaning

Directions: Choose a new vocabulary word from a historical or scientific text. Compete the *Frayer Model* below to show understanding of the vocabulary word.

Text: _____

Author: _____

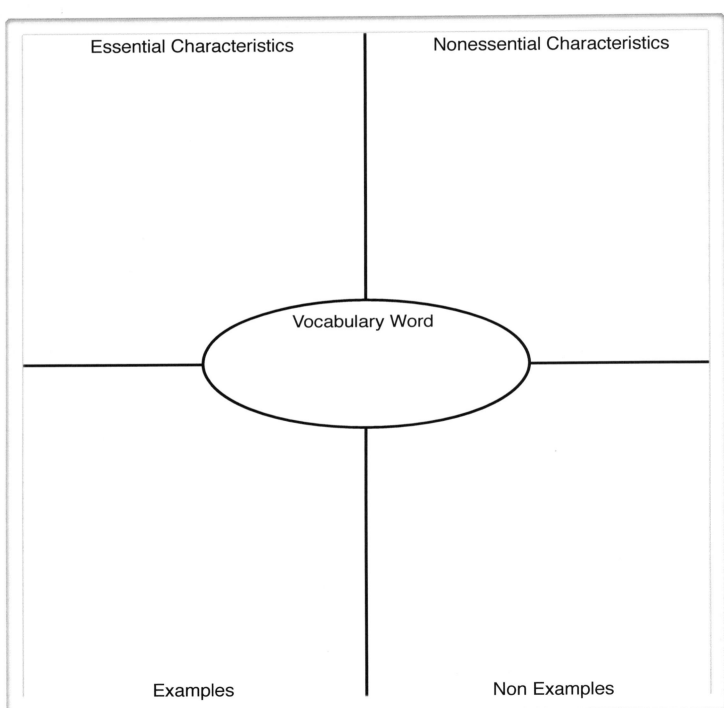

Essential Characteristics	Nonessential Characteristics

Vocabulary Word

Examples	Non Examples

Name: _____

Associations

Directions: To review the topic being discussed in class, use the cluster map below. Write the topic in the center. Them write words or phrases associated with the topic all around.

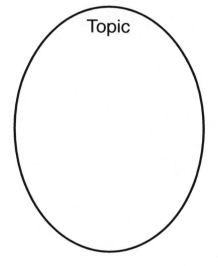

Topic

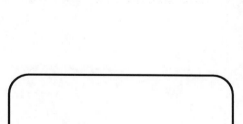

Name: _____

Problem/Solution

Directions: One of the overall text structures found in informational text is problem/solution. Read a selection of informational text. Look for signal words in the text, such as *problem, issue, since, as a result, idea, leads to,* and *causes.* Ask yourself what the problem is, and what the solution is.

Text: _____

Author: _____

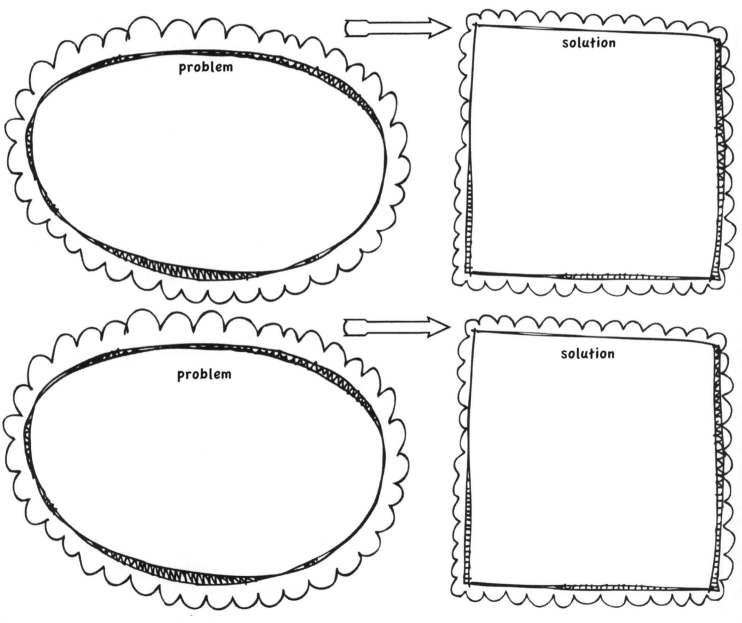

Level: Fourth Grade   Name: _____

Problem/Solution

Directions: One of the overall text structures found in informational text is cause/effect. Read a selection of informational text. Look for signal words in the text, such as *if/then, as a result, because, since, due to,* and *therefore.* What is the cause? Is there more than one effect? Sometimes an effect can cause something new to happen. Color the arrows to show the path the cause/effect structure takes.

Text: _____

Author: _____

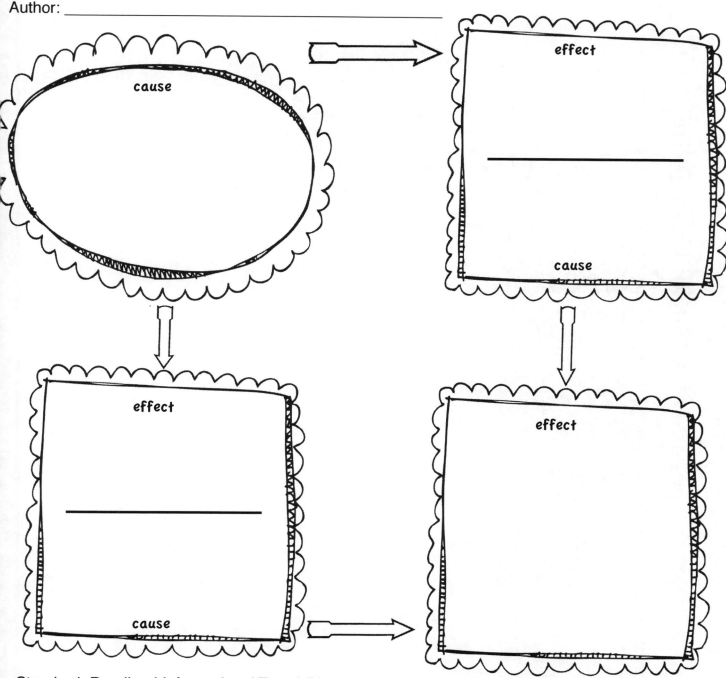

Level: Fourth Grade

Name: _____

Comparing Accounts

Directions: Read two historical texts about the same topic, but told with two different points of view; one by a participant, one by a third party. Then, compare the two texts to see how they are alike and different. Cite examples from the text to support your comparisons.

Historical Topic: _____

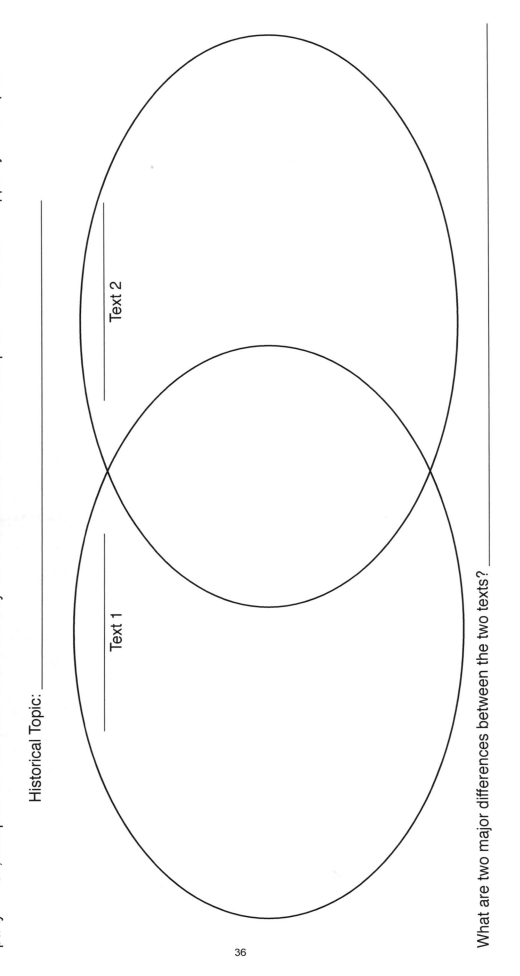

Text 1

Text 2

What are two major differences between the two texts?

_____

_____

36

Standard: Reading I Informational Text I RI.4.6

Level: Fourth Grade

Name: _____

Comparing Accounts

Directions: Using the internet, and newspaper and magazine articles, compare and contrast a chosen topic. Complete the chart below to compare the different accounts of the topic. Select points or events from the topic upon which to focus and compare.

Topic: _____

Resources: _____

Event or Point	Account 1 _____	Account 2 _____
1.		
2.		
3.		

Why might the accounts differ at times? _____

Standard: Reading I Informational Text I RI.4.6

©http://CoreCommonStandards.com

Name: _____

Visual and Oral Interpretations

Directions: Sometimes seeing a speech being given and hearing the words can have a different impact than just reading them. Read President Franklin D. Roosevelt's address to Congress on December 8, 1941, a day after the attack on Pearl Harbor. Then, watch or listen to the actual speech spoken by the President.

Compare the versions. Does hearing or seeing the President actually speak make you feel differently about the words? Does hearing his voice and the tone in witch he speaks help you better understand the severity of the words? Write similarities and differences between the versions of this famous speech.

President Franklin D Roosevelt's Address to the Nation
December 8, 1941

Written Speech	Audio/Video of Actual Speech

You Tube Video of President Roosevelt's Address
http://www.youtube.com/watch?v=3VqQAf74fsE

Original Speech
Bold type words are presented in the video.
Italicized words are omitted from video.

Mr. Vice President, Mr. Speaker, Members of the Senate, and of the House of Representatives:
Yesterday, December 7th, 1941 -- a date which will live in infamy -- the United States of America was suddenly and deliberately attacked by naval and air forces of the Empire of Japan.
The United States was at peace with that nation and, at the solicitation of Japan, was still in conversation with its government and its emperor looking toward the maintenance of peace in the Pacific.
Indeed, one hour after Japanese air squadrons had commenced bombing in the American island of Oahu, the Japanese ambassador to the United States and his colleague delivered to our Secretary of State a formal reply to a recent American message. *And while this reply stated that it seemed useless to continue the existing diplomatic negotiations, it contained no threat or hint of war or of armed attack.*
It will be recorded that the distance of Hawaii from Japan makes it obvious that the attack was deliberately planned many days or even weeks ago. During the intervening time, the Japanese government has deliberately sought to deceive the United States by false statements and expressions of hope for continued peace.

The attack yesterday on the Hawaiian islands has caused severe damage to American naval and military forces. I regret to tell you that very many American lives have been lost. In addition, American ships have been reported torpedoed on the high seas between San Francisco and Honolulu.
Yesterday, the Japanese government also launched an attack against Malaya. Last night, Japanese forces attacked Hong Kong. Last night, Japanese forces attacked Guam. Last night, Japanese forces attacked the Philippine Islands.
Last night, the Japanese attacked Wake Island.
And this morning, the Japanese attacked Midway Island.
Japan has, therefore, undertaken a surprise offensive extending throughout the Pacific area. The facts of yesterday and today speak for themselves. *The people of the United States have already formed their opinions and well understand the implications to the very life and safety of our nation.*
As commander in chief of the Army and Navy, I have directed that all measures be taken for our defense. But always will our whole nation remember the character of the onslaught against us.
No matter how long it may take us to overcome this premeditated invasion, the American people in their righteous might will win through to absolute victory.
I believe that I interpret the will of the Congress and of the people when I assert that we will not only defend ourselves to the uttermost, but will make it very certain that this form of treachery shall never again endanger us.
Hostilities exist. There is no blinking at the fact that our people, our territory, and our interests are in grave danger.
With confidence in our armed forces, with the unbounding determination of our people, we will gain the inevitable triumph -- so help us God.
I ask that the Congress declare that since the unprovoked and dastardly attack by Japan on Sunday, December 7th, 1941, a state of war has existed between the United States and the Japanese empire.

Name: _____

Biographical Time Line

Directions: Read a biography of a historical individual. Use the time line below to record the significant events of the person's life. Write a brief summary of the individual.

Biography _____ Author(s) _____

Begin

End

40

Standard: Reading | Informational Text | RI.4.7

Level: Fourth Grade   Name: _____

Building Knowledge Through Evidence

Directions: Read an informational text on a chosen topic. Complete the three-column notes chart below to help you better understand the content. Begin by writing information you know about the topic. Then, as you read, write facts that add to your background knowledge. Finally, write how your thinking may have changed based on the new facts.

Topic: _____

Text: _____

Author: _____

Background Knowledge	Text Clues	Inferences

Standard: Reading I Informational Text I RI.4.8

Name: _____

Supporting Points

Directions: Read about a famous person or a historical event. Write a diary entry from the point of view of someone who witnessed the event or as the person from the biography. Use evidence from the text to support a particular view or point.

Text: _____

Author: _____

Dear Diary, _____

_____

_____

_____

_____

_____

_____

_____

_____

_____

_____

_____

_____

Name: _____

Integrating Knowledge

Directions: Read two different texts, preferably in two different forms (ex: poem, essay, story, reference), on the same topic. Write key information from both sources. Combine the information to form a better understanding of the topic. Share your new knowledge with someone.

_____
Topic

_____
Text

_____
Text

Name: _____

The Future Me

Directions: What do you want to be when you grow up? Use different informational sources to research a particular career you might like to pursue.   Using informational text features, create a poster that provides information about the career and entices others to learn more about it.

Name: _____

The Future Me

Directions: What do you want to be when you grow up? Use different informational sources to research a particular career you might like to pursue.   Using informational text features, create a poster that provides information about the career and entices others to learn more.

What resources did you use to find out more about the career you chose?

_____

_____

_____

_____

_____

Why did you choose this career?

_____

_____

_____

_____

_____

_____

Did you find out anything new about this career?

_____

_____

_____

_____

Standard: Reading I Informational Text I RI.4.9
Graphics (c) ScrappinDoodles   ©http://CoreCommonStandards.com

Name: _____

Nonfiction I Am Reading

Directions: Keep track of the nonfiction text you read this year in Fourth Grade. When you finish a book, write the title and the date you completed the book. What was the topic?

Date	Book Title	Topic

Level: Fourth Grade   Name: _____

What Are They Reading?

Directions: Keep track of the nonfiction text your students can read this year at grade level. Write the date each type of text was read successfully.

Name	nonfiction storybook	photo-graphic essay	auto-biography	informational book	journal/ diary

Standard: Reading I Informational Text I RI.4.10   ©http://CoreCommonStandards.com

Multi-syllabic Words

Directions: Read the multi-syllabic words below. Write the words so that each is split into its proper syllables. Then, color 3-syllable words yellow, 4-syllable words pink, and 5-syllable words blue.

ex: cornucopia	corn-u-co-pi-a
cooperate	co-op-er-ate
obstacle	ob-st-acle
geography	geo-graph-y
permission	per-mis-sion
exercise	ex-erc.se
individual	indi-vid-ual
character	character
synthesis	synthesis
dynamite	dynamite
harmonica	harm-onica
particular	part-ic+ular
democracy	dem-oc-ra.cy

Name: _____

Multi-syllabic Science Words

Directions: Read the multi-syllabic science words below. Write the words so that each is split into its proper syllables. Then, color 3-syllable words yellow, 4-syllable words pink, and 5-syllable words blue.

ex: cornucopia	corn-u-co-pi-a
investigate	in-ves-ti-gate
hypothesize	hypothesize
chemical	chem-ical
camouflage	cam-ou-flage
conclusion	con-clus-ion
oceanic	ocean-ic
scientist	sci-ent-ist
nonrenewable	non-renew-able
constellation	con-stell-ation
supernatural	super-nat-ural
classification	class-if-ic-ation

Name: _____

Reading With Fluency

fiction

Directions: When you read, you are not just saying the words. Readers read with a purpose and to understand. Practice reading orally so that you can be a fluent reader.
Read the passage below while your teacher times you. Try to read as many words accurately as you can in one minute. Try again in a couple of weeks to see if your fluency improves. {Goal of 140 WPM}

Pick Me!

Eddie really liked to play dodgeball. He was not the tallest kid, and he was not the biggest kid. He was not the fastest kid, and he was not the slowest kid. He was the kid with the best hands.
When his classmates chose teammates for dodgeball, they liked to pick the fast kids first, because they were good at dodging. Then they would pick the kids with the strong arms, because they were good at getting people out when they threw a ball. Everyone else came after that.
Eddie usually got picked last, and it made him sad. Maybe if he was taller or faster, it would have helped. He couldn't help that, but he could do his best. He would have to show them that his talents made for a good team.
When the game started, the fast kids ran forward and grabbed the balls first. They threw them, and several people on each team were eliminated. Then, the strong arms came in handy. The boys with the best arms could whiz the dodgeballs across the court. It stung if one of them hit you.
Some of the big kids went down first. They made easy targets. The fast kids fell eventually, too. That left Eddie standing alone on the court for his team, holding a red rubber ball. He smiled, even though his teammates groaned to see him facing four enemies on his own. "Not Eddie." They whined, thinking he was useless, but he would show them.
When one of the strong arms on the other team threw a ball, he deflected it with his own and tagged him out with his ball. Now there were only three left on the other team. The odds were more even now. He got another ball and approached the center line. A fast kid charged at him, throwing the ball low. Eddie dropped his own ball and caught the other kid's ball. The fast kid was out, and he got one of his teammates back. "John, you're in!" Eddie shouted over his shoulder.
Everyone watched in surprise. Now it was two-on-two. Eddie and John each got a ball, sighted in the slow kid on the other team and fired. Eddie missed, but his shot led the other player right into John's shot. Now it was two-to-one.
It didn't take long to finish off the last kid. Eddie was a hero. His team rushed in to cheer for him. They wouldn't be picking him last anymore.

Date	Words Read Correctly Per Minute

Standard: Reading I Foundational Skills I RF.4.4

©http://CoreCommonStandards.com

Name: _____

Reading With Fluency

nonfiction

Directions: When you read, you are not just saying the words. Readers read with a purpose and to understand. Practice reading orally so that you can be a fluent reader.
Read the passage below while your teacher times you. Try to read as many words accurately as you can in one minute. Try again in a couple of weeks to see if your fluency improves. {Goal of 140 WPM}

Poison Dart Frogs

Poison dart frogs wear some of the most brilliant and beautiful colors on Earth. Depending on their habitats, which are from the tropical forests of Costa Rica to Brazil, their coloring can be yellow, gold, copper, red, green, blue, or black. Their designs and colors scare off predators.

You may have seen monkeys carrying their children on their backs. Well, some of these frogs show some of these parenting habits, including carrying both eggs and tadpoles on their backs.

These frogs are some of the most toxic animals on Earth. The two-inch-long Golden Poison Dart Frog has enough venom to kill 10 grown men. Indigenous people of Colombia have used its powerful venom for centuries to tip their blowgun darts when hunting.

Scientists are not sure why these poison dart frogs are so poisonous, but it is possible they take in plant poisons which are carried by their prey, including ants, termites and beetles. Poison dart frogs raised in captivity and isolated from insects in their native habitat never develop venom. The medical research community has been exploring ways to use poison dart frog venom in medicine. Scientists have already used their venom to create a painkiller medicine.

Date	Words Read Correctly Per Minute

Name: _____

Supporting an Opinion

Directions: Write a piece that expresses your opinion about a topic you are discussing in class. Provide reasons and include facts and details that support your opinion. Link the reasons and opinions using words such as *for instance, in order to, and in addition*. Write a concluding statement.

Topic: _____

My Opinion

[ ]

Reason	Reason	Reason	Reason

facts and details	facts and details	facts and details	facts and details

Concluding Statement: _____

_____

_____

_____

_____

Standard: Reading I Writing I W.4.1

Level: Fourth Grade   Name: _____

Supporting an Opinion

Directions: Write a piece that expresses your opinion about a topic you are discussing in class. Provide reasons and include facts and details that support your opinion. Link the reasons and opinions using words such as *for instance, in order to, and in addition.*

Topic: _____

My Opinion: _____

_____

_____

Reason #1:

_____

_____

Supporting Evidence _____

_____

_____

Reason #2:

_____

_____

Supporting Evidence _____

_____

_____

Reason #3:

_____

_____

Supporting Evidence _____

_____

_____

Reason #4:

_____

_____

Supporting Evidence _____

_____

_____

Name: _____

To Inform and Explain

Directions: Write an informative text grouping related information in paragraphs. Develop the topic with facts and details. Use vocabulary related to the topic, and write a concluding sentence.

_____

_____

_____

_____

_____

_____

_____

_____

_____

_____

_____

_____

_____

_____

_____

_____

_____

Name: _____

_____

_____

_____

_____

_____

_____

_____

_____

_____

_____

_____

_____

_____

_____

Name: _____

Informational Paragraph

Directions: Choose a topic. Write about that topic in a way that informs or explains. Write what you know about the topic and what you learned after researching. Record facts and other information to help support your writing. Write a paragraph below.

What I Know	**What I Have Learned**

facts/definitions/details/other information

Write an informative paragraph...

_____

_____

_____

_____

_____

_____

_____

_____

Name: _____

Real Life Narrative

Directions: Think about an experience you have had in your life. It may be a positive experience, or perhaps, a negative one. Cite the situation and choose a narrator to tell the story. Describe the narrator and how he or she is related to the situation. Sequence events and write key dialogue that will take place in the story. Write a conclusion. Rewrite the story as a narrative.

situation

narrator

Event	Event	Event
_____	_____	_____
_____	_____	_____
_____	_____	_____

key dialogue

conclusion

©http://CoreCommonStandards.com

Fictional Narrative

Directions: Create an experience you have wanted to have in your life. Cite the situation and choose a narrator to tell the story. Describe the narrator and how he or she is related to the situation. Sequence events and write key dialogue that will take place in the story. Describe the events. Write a conclusion, then rewrite the story as a narrative.

situation

narrator

Event	Event	Event
_____	_____	_____
_____	_____	_____
_____	_____	_____
_____	_____	_____

key dialogue

conclusion

Name: _____

Writing in Fourth Grade

Directions: Choose a format, pick a topic, and write. Be aware of the expectations in fourth grade writing.

 # Opinion Piece

My topic:

My position:

 # Informative/Explanatory Piece

My topic:

My purpose:

 # Narrative Piece

My topic:

My audience:

Name: _____

Writing in Fourth Grade

Directions: Produce writing that demonstrates the development and organization expected in fourth grade.

Write opinion pieces

☐ Introduce the topic

☐ State an opinion

☐ Create an organized structure with related ideas grouped to support purpose

☐ Provide a concluding statement

Write informative/explanatory text

☐ Introduce the topic

☐ Group related information together in paragraphs and sections

☐ Include illustrations when useful

☐ Develop the topic with facts, definitions, details, quotations, and other information

☐ Connect ideas with linking words (also, another, and, more, but)

☐ Use domain-specific vocabulary

☐ Provide a concluding statement

Write narratives of real or imaginary events

☐ Establish a situation

☐ Introduce a narrator and/or characters

☐ Organize an event sequence that unfolds naturally

☐ Use dialogue and descriptions of actions, thoughts, and feelings

☐ Use transitional and concrete words and phrases to sequence events

☐ Provide a conclusion

Standard: Reading I Writing I W.4.4

Editors

Directions: After completing a piece of writing, use this chart to edit your writing for spelling and other conventions. Work with a partner...maybe they will see something you missed. Fix your errors. Think about why they needed to be corrected.

Mark	Description	Example
∧	insert	is What time dinner? ∧ Is this for the tree 'or for the flowers? ∧
☰	capitalize	Sanchez lives in poland. ≡
⌗	add space	⌗ Betty dancedwith her troupe. ∧
✗	delete	She went with ~~with~~ him to the beach.
⌒	close space	The beetle ate ⌒ the aphid.
¶	new paragraph	So they sat on the porch and watched the parade. ¶ The next week, Danny and Paul went for a long trip on their canoe.
ⓢⓟ	spelling error	ⓢⓟ Papa likes to golg in the morning.
∼	transpose	Diane and friend her sewed a blanket.
⊙	add period	Mom likes her coffee in the morning⊙ She puts coffee in for her.

Name: _____

Revising

Directions: After completing a piece of writing, use this chart to revise your writing. Work with a partner...maybe they will see something you missed. Improve your writing. Listen to how it sounds.

☐ 1. Does the beginning grab (or hook) the reader's attention?

☐ 2. Are all of the possible questions answered?
Did I answer Who? What? Where? When? Why? How?

☐ 3. Are my words interesting? Should I change one for another?

☐ 4. Is there enough detail to express feelings and thoughts?

☐ 5. Do I need to add more details, reasons, or examples?

☐ 6. Have I used enough descriptive words so the reader can picture what I am writing about?

☐ 7. Do I use varied sentence beginnings?

☐ 8. Did I use figurative language such as similes, metaphors, vivid verbs, onomatopoeia, and adjectives?

☐ 9. Do my sentences stay focused on the topic?

☐ 10. Does the writing flow sequentially?

☐ 11. Does the ending bring the piece to a close?

Name: _____

Using Technology

Directions: Use the computer to create, publish and present a piece of writing.

My topic is...

_____

I am going to use a computer to create my story.

I will enhance my writing by using...

a. *digital camera,* b. *scanner,* c. *clipart website.*

I will share my writing by...

a. *printing my story*
b. *emailing it to my classmates*
c. *presenting it using a projector*
d. *creating a powerpoint presentation*
e. *movie-making program*
f. *other:*_____

computer tools

spell check
font
word art

online tools

thesaurus
dictionary
clipart
animation

writing checklist

prewriting		
drafting		
revising		
word choice		
sentence structure		
editing		
punctuation		
capitalization		
spelling		

What I need to add/change/delete...

_____

_____

_____

_____

_____

_____

_____

Standard: Reading I Writing I W.4.6

©http://CoreCommonStandards.com

Name: _____

Using Digital Resources

Directions: It is important today for students to learn to use digital tools to write. Use this checklist to record what digital skills each student can perform.

Digital Skill	Date	Success
Uses a mouse well. (Can double-click; move cursor to desired place; scroll if available.)		
Knows where all common characters are on keyboard.		
Knows how to use space bar; back space; delete; and return.		
Can log in and out of programs.		
Can change the font or size of font.		
Can add a graphic.		
Can drag and drop an item.		
Can copy/paste an item.		
Can save a file.		
Can print work.		
Can create a Powerpoint Presentation.		
Can locate information on the internet.		
Can send an email.		
Can attach a file to an email.		
Has sufficient command of keyboarding skills to type a minimum of one page in a single sitting		

Standard: Reading I Writing I W.4.6   ©http://CoreCommonStandards.com

Name: _____

Research Projects

Directions: Conduct a research project on The Civil War. Explain the reasons the Civil War began, some of the important people of the war, and the most important battles.

The Civil War began on _____ and ended on _____.

The main reasons the Civil War began were: _____

_____

_____

_____

_____

_____

_____

The important people of the Civil War: _____

_____

_____

_____

_____

_____

The major battles of the Civil War: _____

_____

_____

_____

_____

_____

_____

_____

Level: Fourth Grade   Name: _____

Research Projects

Directions: Choose a topic to research. Use various research tools to learn about your topic and obtain information to present to others. Include a bibliography to cite your resources. Use this sheet to help you write your bibliography.

For a Book:
Author Name: _____,_____
                          (last)   (first)   (second name or initial)

Second Author: _____,_____
                          (last)   (first)   (second name or initial)

Title Underlined: _____

Location Book was Published: _____

Publisher Name: _____

Copyright Date: _____

Example: Cox, Clinton. <u>Mark Twain America's Humorist, Dreamer, Prophet: a Biography.</u>
       New York Scholastic, 1995.

_____

_____

For the Internet:

Author Name: _____,_____
                          (last)   (first)   (second name or initial)

Second Author: _____,_____
                          (last)   (first)   (second name or initial)

Web article title in quotes: _____

Website Title Underlined: _____

Date website was accessed by you_____

Website url: _____

Example: Blount, Roy. "Mark Twain: Our Original Superstar." <u>Time Magazine U.S.</u> 2008.
      Time Magazine Online. 3 July, 2008. http://www.time.com/time/magazine/article/0,9171,1820166,00.html

Standard: Reading I Writing I W.4.7   ©http://CoreCommonStandards.com
66

Name: _____

Taking Notes

Directions: Use printed or digital resources to gather information on a chosen topic. Take notes and categorize the information.   Cite the resources you used.

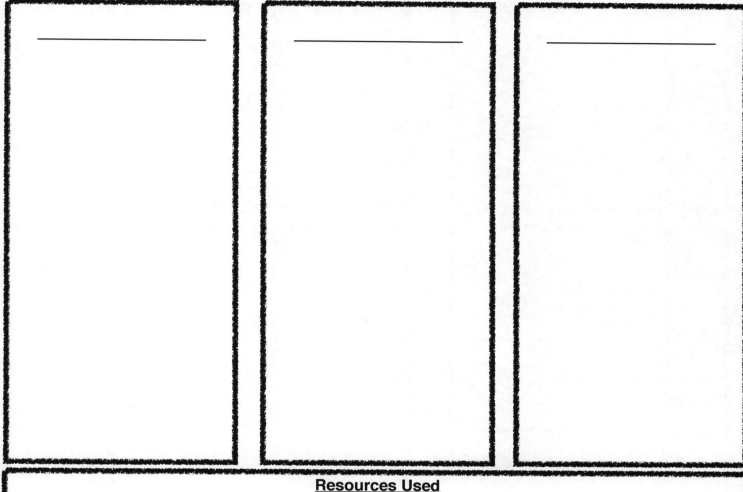

Resources Used

Name: _____

Taking Notes

Directions: Use printed or digital resources to gather information on a chosen topic. Take notes and categorize the information.   Cite the resources you used.

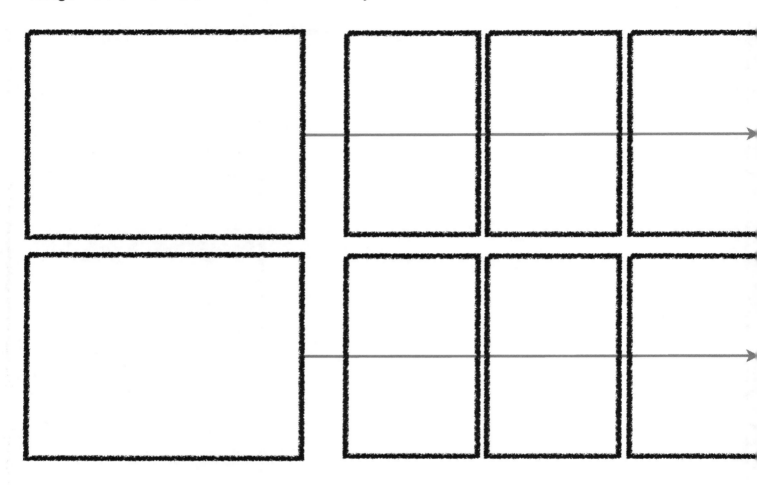

Resources Used

©http://CoreCommonStandards.com

Name: _____

Character Analysis

Directions: After reading a literary story or drama, describe in depth a character from the text. Think about the character's words, thoughts, and actions throughout the text. Use evidence from the text to support your analysis of the character. Write a short character analysis.

Title & Author

Character

Description	Description	Description

Evidence	Evidence	Evidence

Analysis

Reasons and Evidence

Directions: After reading an informational text, choose a point the author is trying to make in the text. Write the reasons and evidence the author uses to support his or her point.

Title & Author

Main Point

reasons that support the point	reasons that support the point

Evidence   Evidence   Evidence

Conclusion

Name: _____

Writing in Different Genres

Directions: Use this chart to record the types of writing you do, the dates, the audience, and the purpose for the writing.

Writing Genre	Date	Audience	Purpose
Journal Entry			
Scientific Research Paper			
Historical Research paper			
Biography			
Autobiography			
Poem			
Song			
Adventure Story			
Realistic Fiction			
Nonfiction Story			
Informational Writing			
Procedural Writing			
Interview			
News Story			
Letter			
Reflection			

Standard: Reading I Writing I W.4.10

Level: Fourth Grade   Name: _____

Daily Writing

Directions: *When writers write, we sometimes spend several days, or even weeks, working on a particular piece. Sometimes, a piece of writing may be completed in only a few hours, or minutes. Writers write for many reasons. But no matter what is written, the writer should think about the purpose of the piece, and the audience...or who will be reading it.*

Use this chart to keep track of writing you complete. Try to vary the genres and disciplines (subjects) in which you write. Keep in mind the purpose and audience for each piece.

Title of Piece/Genre	Date	Audience	Purpose

Standard: Reading I Writing I W.4.10

Level: Fourth Grade   Name: _____

Collaborative Discussions

Directions: Fourth graders meet in groups to discuss various topics. Use this sheet to record times you gather in discussion groups.

format: one-on-one / group / teacher-led

date:

topic:

what I did to prepare:

questions I asked:

comments I made:

something I learned:

---

format: one-on-one / group / teacher-led

date:

topic:

what I did to prepare:

questions I asked:

comments I made:

something I learned:

Name: _____

Paraphrasing

Paraphrasing is the act of borrowing a passage from another source and rewriting it in your own words. The meaning of the passage should remain the same, but told in your own words and voice. Giving credit to the original source is important.

Directions: After listening to a selected text read aloud, or information presented in some form of media, paraphrase the information below. Write the main idea to help you organize your thoughts.

Main Idea

Paraphrase

_____

_____

_____

_____

_____

_____

_____

_____

_____

_____

Standard: Reading I Speaking & Listening I SL.4.2

Name: _____

Listening for Reasons

Directions: Listen to a guest speaker talk about a particular topic. Identify the key points the speaker is trying to make. Write the points, and the evidence and reasons the speaker uses to support the points.

Key Points

Reasons and Evidence

Reasons and Evidence

Name: _____

Speaking of...

Directions: Choose a topic or text on which to report or recount an experience. Organize your ideas, include facts and descriptive detail to support the main ideas or themes.
Present your information orally. Speak clearly at an understandable pace.

What I am presenting: _____

My main points:

Facts, evidence, reasons, details:

Parts of my presentation on which I want to place the most emphasis:

Standard: Reading I Speaking & Listening I SL.4.4   ©http://CoreCommonStandards.com
Graphics (c) ScrappinDoodles

Adding Audio and Visual Components

Directions: Add audio recordings and/or visual displays to a presentation to enhance the development of the main ideas.   Use a computer, iPod, iPad, or digital recorder to record your voice. Include photographs, clipart, and other digital graphics. Use fluid reading and speak with interest in order to express emphasize or enhance certain facts or details. Don't forget to include your own point of view.

There are several programs available for children to use to create digital stories. Some are listed below.

For Microsoft Products
Photostory ...free program using still photos or graphics and added audio

Powerpoint

For Apple Products
My Story-Book Maker ...App for iPad/iPod/iPhone ($)
        make drawings and record your voice

Writer's Studio ...App for iPad/iPod/iPhone ($)
        make drawings, add photos, and record your voice

iMovie ...usually included in Mac purchase

Keynote (like Powerpoint) included in iWorks

Use clipart and paint programs, scanners, digital cameras, and digital pens to create and include graphics and visual displays.

My Presentation:

_____

_____

_____

Components I will add...

_____ computer graphics   _____ songs   _____ different font

_____ scanned photographs   _____ speeches   _____ bold, italic, underline

_____ scanned drawings   _____ audio text   _____ movie/TV clips

_____ computer drawings   _____ sound effects   _____ video

Name: _____

Formal vs Informal

Directions: When do we use formal language? When do we use informal language? Look at the activities below. Think about the setting and who is involved. Write if the activity would use formal or informal language.

When you speak daily, keep in mind when you should use formal English, and when an informal discourse is appropriate.

small group discussion	phone a friend	share a book report
_____	_____	_____
explain a procedure	phone call to the bank	email a family member
_____	_____	_____
write a text message	apply for a job	write a letter to a business
_____	_____	_____
share a joke with a friend	meet your friend's parents	make a speech
_____	_____	_____
leave a phone message at the doctor's	give instructions	write in your journal
_____	_____	_____

Prepositional Phrases

Directions: Complete the sentences with the best prepositional phrase from the box below

into the house	beyond the trees	by accident	within one's rights
for a change	on the horizon	out of respect	under discussion

1. I asked mom if she and dad had decided yet, but she said the topic was still

_____.

2. Carl was supposed to buy dill pickles, but he bought sweet pickles

_____.

3. It is _____ to decide whether or not to

go to college.

4. The ball Paul kicked sailed _____.

5. It started raining, so we decided to the move the party

_____.

6. I thought maybe instead of peanut butter and jelly, I would have peanut butter

and cheese _____.

7. From the dock, we looked out _____ and

could see the Tall Ships in the distance.

8. _____ for the soldiers in the parade, we stood

silent and lifted our hands to our hearts.

Picking the Right Word

Directions: Complete each sentence with the best word from the box below.

to	**too**	**two**	**your**	**you're**
their	**they're**	**there**	**where**	**wear**	**we're**

1. I don't know _____ we are going _____ find a new cat.

2. I will _____ a coat if you do _____ .

3. _____ going to play outside in _____ sandbox.

4. Can I use _____ markers while _____ at school?

5. _____ are _____ movies that _____ going to see

Directions: Complete the sentences below by adding text to the beginning or ending of each.

and they all rolled down the hill

_____

One day last week

_____

went over to the store

_____

My mom and my sister

_____

Name: _____

Auxiliary Verbs

Directions: Complete the sentences with the correct auxiliary (helping) verb. Fill in the blank and circle the correct verb.

1. Grandma said she isn't certain, but we _____ be going to Disney!

   may   will   would

2. Mom will be home soon so we _____ get our rooms cleaned!

   could   should   would

3. Sophie told me that she _____ handle the uneven bars in gymnastics.

   could   have to   ought to

4. Dad said, that before I play outside, I _____ do my homework.

   may   would   had better

5. Carter _____ go with me to the store if I buy him a snack.

   might   should   can

6. I _____ try hard this year in school.

   would   will   shall

7. If we studied for the test, we probably _____ have passed.

   will   would   ought to

Name: _____

Fixing Punctuation

Directions: Read the text below. Correct the words that need capital letters, insert proper apostrophes {'}, and add the correct punctuation at the end. { . ! ? }

On July 4 1884 France gave the United States an amazing birthday gift: the Statue of Liberty Without the base at the bottom, it is as tall as a 15-story building. she is a symbol of the united states But the world-famous statue of liberty standing in new york harbor was built in france The statue was shown to the U.S., taken apart shipped across the Atlantic Ocean in crates, and rebuilt in the U.S. it was frances gift to the american people.

It all started at dinner one night near paris in 1865. A group of frenchmen were talking about their dictator and the democratic government of the U.S. they wanted to build a monument to support American freedom Maybe then, France would have a democracy in their own country at that dinner was the sculptor Frédéric-Auguste bartholdi He imagined a statue of a woman holding a torch burning with the light of freedom. it took 21 years for this idea to become a reality. french supporters raised money to build the statue and americans paid for the base it would stand on. finally in 1886 the statue was dedicated

Fixing Punctuation

Directions: Read the text below. Correct the words that need capital letters, insert proper apostrophes {'} , and add the correct punctuation at the end. { . ! ? }

Answer Key

   On July 4, 1884 France gave the United States an amazing birthday gift: the Statue of Liberty! Without the base at the bottom, it is as tall as a 15-story building. She is a symbol of the United States. But the world-famous Statue of Liberty standing in New York Harbor was built in France. The statue was shown to the U.S., taken apart, shipped across the Atlantic Ocean in crates, and rebuilt in the U.S. It was France's gift to the American people.

   It all started at dinner one night near Paris in 1865. A group of Frenchmen were talking about their dictator and the democratic government of the U.S. They wanted to build a monument to support American freedom. Maybe then, France would have a democracy in their own country. At that dinner was the sculptor Frédéric-Auguste Bartholdi. He imagined a statue of a woman holding a torch burning with the light of freedom. It took 21 years for this idea to become a reality. French supporters raised money to build the statue, and Americans paid for the base it would stand on. Finally, in 1886, the statue was dedicated.

Fixing Punctuation

Directions: Read the text below. Correct the words that need capital letters, insert proper apostrophes {'} and quotation marks {""} , and add the correct punctuation at the end. { . ! ? }

Welcome to the Neighborhood

The old roger house had been empty for six months and finally someone was moving in Betsy didn't see any children getting out of the car, just an older woman in a wheelchair. betsy thought she is going to be lonely by herself. The moving men brought all the furniture into the house the lady didn't have too many things Betsy started feeling sorry for her. Mom, is it alright if I go over to say hello to our new neighbor   "Why don't you wait until tomorrow? Give her a chance to get settled.

the next morning they decided to bring some cookies to their new neighbor and introduce themselves the lady came to the door and said her name was emily harris. she invited them into the house. Please forgive the way the house looks, said Miss Harris. "I haven't had much time to put things away and being in a wheelchair makes it twice as hard." betsy and her mom introduced themselves and stayed only for a short time. We don't want to hold you up, said Betsy's mom. "If you ever need anything, let us know" "Thanks so much" said Miss Harris

after breakfast the next day Betsy decided she wanted to help miss harris get settled in It was Saturday, so she had all day. Betsy really liked Miss harris. Betsy rang the doorbell but didn't get an answer. The door was unlocked so Betsy peeked in only to see Miss Harris had tried to reach a shelf and had taken a fall next to her wheelchair Betsy ran to Miss Harris and asked her if she was alright. I think I broke my arm, said Miss Harris. "I'll be right back," said Betsy she ran home and told her mom. they called for an ambulance. they arrived shortly and took Miss Harris to the hospital While Miss Harris was gone betsy decided to unpack the boxes that were on the floor and put things away to surprise and help Miss Harris once she returned home She was going to need a lot of help now that she broke her arm When miss Harris returned home on sunday she was surprised by Betsy's hard work. You are a very kind girl, said Miss Harris. "I'm so lucky to have bought this house next to you " Betsy smiled the biggest smile and said "Welcome to the neighborhood.

Name: _____

Fixing Punctuation

Directions: Read the text below. Correct the words that need capital letters, insert proper apostrophes {'} , and add the correct punctuation at the end. { . ! ? }

Welcome to the Neighborhood

The old Roger house had been empty for six months, and finally someone was moving in. Betsy didn't see any children getting out of the car, just an older woman in a wheelchair. Betsy thought, she is going to be lonely by herself. The moving men brought all the furniture into the house. The lady didn't have too many things. Betsy started feeling sorry for her. "Mom, is it alright if I go over to say hello to our new neighbor?" "Why don't you wait until tomorrow?" "Give her a chance to get settled."

The next morning they decided to bring some cookies to their new neighbor and introduce themselves. The lady came to the door and said her name was Emily Harris. She invited them into the house. "Please forgive the way the house looks," said Miss Harris. "I haven't had much time to put things away and being in a wheelchair makes it twice as hard." Betsy and her mom introduced themselves and stayed only for a short time. "We don't want to hold you up," said Betsy's mom. "If you ever need anything, let us know." "Thanks so much," said Miss Harris.

After breakfast the next day, Betsy decided she wanted to help Miss Harris get settled in. It was Saturday, so she had all day. Betsy really liked Miss Harris. Betsy rang the doorbell but didn't get an answer. The door was unlocked, so Betsy peeked in only to see Miss Harris had tried to reach a shelf and had taken a fall next to her wheelchair. Betsy ran to Miss Harris and asked her if she was alright. "I think I broke my arm," said Miss Harris. "I'll be right back," said Betsy. She ran home and told her mom. They called for an ambulance. They arrived shortly and took Miss Harris to the hospital. While Miss Harris was gone, Betsy decided to unpack the boxes that were on the floor and put things away to surprise and help Miss Harris once she returned home. She was going to need a lot of help now that she broke her arm. When Miss Harris returned home on Sunday, she was surprised by Betsy's hard work. "You are a very kind girl," said Miss Harris. "I'm so lucky to have bought this house next to you!" Betsy smiled the biggest smile and said, "Welcome to the neighborhood."

Name: _____

Fixing Sentences

Directions: Read the sentences below. Correct the words that need capital letters, insert proper apostrophes {'} and quotation marks {" "} , and add the correct punctuation at the end. { . ! ? }

1	the boston tea party occurred on december 16 1773
2	paul revere made his famous ride to lexington on tuesday april 18 1775
3	george washington took command of the continental army on july 3 1775
4	benjamin franklin was known to say by failing to prepare, you are preparing to fail
5	the continental congress adopted the declaration of independence on july 4 1776
6	john hancocks signature is the most famous one on the declaration of independence
7	did you know that british soldiers were called red coats due to the color of their uniforms
8	george washington is known to have said it is better to be alone than in bad company
9	the largest city in america in 1775 was philadelphia
10	people that continued to support the king of england were called loyalists

Level: Fourth Grade   Name: _____

Punctuating Sentences

Directions: Insert punctuation in the sentences below. Choose punctuation that helps enhance the sentence. Then, rewrite each sentence with correct punctuation on the lines below.

' apostrophe	: colon	, comma
? question mark	! exclamation point	. period
-- dash	" " quotations marks	; semicolon
... ellipsis	- hyphen	( ) parentheses

1. Without hesitating Dudley jumped from the top bleacher and chased down the robber.

_____

_____

2. Well, I finally finished the curtain looks awful but it's finished.

_____

_____

3. I will have three things for lunch ham, cheese, and an apple.

_____

_____

4. Paul and Tom had a fight they aren't talking to each other.

_____

_____

5. Mom said, Please help me bake a cake.

_____

_____

6. I don't have a bicycle, so I am borrowing my cousins.

_____

_____

Name: _____

The Right Punctuation

Directions: Insert punctuation in the sentences below. Choose punctuation that helps enhance the sentence. Then, rewrite each sentence with correct punctuation on the lines below.

' apostrophe	: colon	, comma
? question mark	! exclamation point	. period
-- dash	" " quotations marks	; semicolon
... ellipsis	- hyphen	( ) parentheses

1. How many pies do you have to make for the carnival

   _____

   _____

2. We all hid behind the furniture and yelled surprise

   _____

   _____

3. My brother told me he'd be here when school got out but he never came

   _____

   _____

4. Even though the dog was friendly looking, mom told me not to pet him.

   _____

   _____

5. On the sign were the words Piso Mojado wet floor

   _____

   _____

6. Next Friday is the last day I can buy tickets to the concert

   _____

   _____

Name: _____

Writing with Effect

Directions: Write a sentence to describe each of the pictures below. Use descriptive words and phrases such as adjectives and adverbs, idioms, metaphors, and similes for effect. Insert proper punctuation that helps enhance the sentences.

Name: _____

Formal Language

Directions: Choose the best word to complete the sentences using formal language.

1. I'm afraid we'll have to _____ tomorrow's meeting.

    put off   postpone

2. I am _____ to have the opportunity to work with you.

    grateful   psyched

3. I hope the students will not find the new schedule too _____.

    inconvenient   much of a pain

4. The bank on the corner was _____ in 1956.

    started up   established

5. _____, Thank you for visiting our class last week.

    Hi Mr. Hoosier   Dear Mr. Hoosier

Directions: Circle the words below that would be used in formal language.

contact	started	get	ascertain
make a decision	assist	demonstrate	help
obtain	resolve	tell	find out
commenced	inform	get in touch	show

Name: _____

Using Context Clues

Directions: As you read assigned text, use this form to record unknown words. Write the context clues you used to infer the meaning of the unknown words.

word	clues, inferences meaning:
word	clues, inferences meaning:
word	clues, inferences meaning:
word	clues, inferences meaning:
word	clues, inferences meaning:
word	clues, inferences meaning:

©http://CoreCommonStandards.com

Name: _____

Prefixes and Suffixes

Directions: As you read an assigned text, use this form to record words with Greek and Latin affixes (prefixes and suffixes). Write the affix, and the meaning of the word.

Some examples:

Prefixes: anthro; dem; morph; ped; anti; bio; micro; mono; pan; co; inter; dis; pre; sub; trans

Suffixes: ism; ist; graph; logy; phone; able; fy; port; gress; pend

Word	Affix (prefix or suffix)	Meaning

Level: Fourth Grade   Name: _____

Using Tools to Get Meaning

Directions: As you read assigned text, use this form to record key words. Use dictionaries, glossaries, thesauruses, and other reference tools, both print and digital, to find the pronunciation and meaning of each word.

Word	Pronunciation	Meaning

Standard: Reading I Language I L.4.4   ©http://CoreCommonStandards.com

Name: _____

Adages

Directions: Read the common adages below. Think about the words. Explain what each adage means.

Birds of a feather flock together.	**You can't teach an old dog new tricks.**
A rolling stone gathers no moss.	**Don't judge a book by its cover.**
Two wrongs don't make a right.	**Don't count your chickens before they hatch.**

Name: _____

Matching the Adages

Directions: Read the common adages below. Think about the words. Match each adage on the left to its meaning on the right.

Actions speak louder than words.

A son's character is expected to resemble his father's.

All that glitters is not gold.

Some things sound easy, but in fact are difficult.

Better late than never.

Rumors are usually based on some degree of truth.

Don't put all your eggs in one basket.

What a person actually does is more important than what they say.

It's easier said than done.

Don't express regret over something that has happened and cannot be remedied.

It's no use crying over spilt milk.

It's better to do something, even if it is late, than to not do it at all.

Like father, like son.

Don't invest all your all your efforts into one thing.

Where there's smoke there's fire.

Appearances can be deceptive.

Name: _____

Synonyms & Antonyms

Directions: Match each word in the center to its synonym on the left and its antonym on the right.

produce	**arrive**	unlikely
pollute	**energetic**	purify
doubtful	**create**	lethargic
come	**beneficial**	ignorant
likely	**contaminate**	depart
bright	**probable**	harmful
lively	**dubious**	certain
useful	**intelligent**	destroy

Level: Fourth Grade

Name: _____

Word Study

Directions: Use this semantic map to better understand a key word from your studies. Create symbols, draw pictures, and write words (synonyms) that illustrate the meaning of the word.

Topic of Study: _____

Standard: Reading I Language I L.4.6

Spatial Words

Directions: Choose the best spatial word to fill in each blank below.

1. Susan kicked the football just _____ the goal post.

                onto   **inside**   **apart**

2. My brother was bored so he walked _____ the crowd at the party.

                astride   **amid**   **around**

3. I dropped my coins and some went _____ the sofa.

                between   **beneath**   **aboard**

4. While waiting in line for tickets, I let him cut _____ of me.

                below   **ahead**   **toward**

5. The soldier walked _____ his horse in the parade.

                down   **beyond**   **alongside**

6. I jumped _____ the train just as it was pulling from the track.

                between   **near**   **aboard**

7. If it stops raining, we will place the tables _____ in the yard.

                underneath   **round**   **outside**

8. If you look _____ the bridge, you will see Tom waiting for you.

                away   **amongst**   **across**

Name: _____

Temporal Words

Directions: Choose the best temporal word to fill in each blank below.

1. If I had finished this _____ I could have went skiing today.

prior to   **yesterday**   **formerly**

2. All night I waited for my TV show to start, _____ the President continued to talk on the special news report and I missed it.

however   **meanwhile**   **subsequently**

3. Since we earned the most points, we will get a pizza party _____

never   **tomorrow**   **last night**

4. Unknowingly, she picked up a spider, then she_____ let it go.

immediately   **followed by**   **after**

5. I was awake most of _____, so today I am quite sleepy.

previously   **last night**   **next year**

6. I should have preheated the oven _____ putting in the cake.

before   **followed by**   **first of all**

7. He is _____ enrolled in both high school and community college.

finally   **concurrently**   **prior to**

8. To have the best garden, we till the soil _____.

thereafter   **next**   **yearly**

Standard: Reading I Language I L.4.6

Common Core
State Standards

Fourth Grade Worksheets
Common Core Workbook

Grade 4

•Math Standards

Worksheets that teach every
Common Core Standard!

Name: _____

How Many More Times?

Directions: Solve the multiplicative comparisons. Think about how the numbers relate to one another.

Example: 12 = 4 x 3 because 12 is 4 times as many as 3.

20 = 4 x 5 because 20 is 4 times as many as _____.

14 = 7 x ___ because 14 is ___ times as many as _____.

18 = 9 x ___ because 18 is ___ times as many as _____.

32 = ___ x 4 because ___ is ___ times as many as _____.

27 = ___ x 3 because ___ is ___ times as many as _____.

45 = ___ x 9 because ___ is ___ times as many as _____.

36 = ___ x 12 because ___ is ___ times as many as _____.

81 = ___ x ___ because ___ is ___ times as many as _____.

90 = ___ x ___ because ___ is ___ times as many as _____.

108 = ___ x ___ because ___ is ___ times as many as _____.

Standard: Math I Operations & Algebraic Thinking I 4.OA.1

©www.CoreCommonStandards.com

Name: _____

How Many More Times?

Directions: Read the multiplication equations below. Think about the comparison between the factors. Draw a diagram to show the relationship.

5 x 3 = 15 means 15 is 3 times more than 5.	**4 x 8 = 32 means 32 is 8 times more than 4.**	**6 x 7 = 42 means 42 is 7 times more than 6.**
5 x 6 = 30 means 30 is 6 times more than 5.	**8 x 2 = 16 means 16 is 2 times more than 8.**	**6 x 4 = 24 means 24 is 4 times more than 6.**
3 x 7 = 21 means 21 is 7 times more than 3.	**9 x 8 = 72 means 72 is 8 times more than 9.**	**3 x 9 = 27 means 27 is 9 times more than 3.**
5 x 8 = 40 means 40 is 8 times more than 5.	**9 x 2 = 18 means 18 is 2 times more than 9.**	**8 x 7 = 56 means 56 is 7 times more than 8.**

Name: _____

How Many Times?

Directions: Solve the multiplication problems. You may use drawings and equations to show your work.

Bridget is 6 years old. Her mom is 7 times older than her. How old is Bridget's mom?

_____ years old

_____ x _____ = _____

Courtney has 5 times as many flowers as Hayley. If Hayley has 4 flowers, how many flowers does Courtney have?

_____ flowers

_____ x _____ = _____

The art box I received for Christmas has 63 crayons. It has 9 times more crayons than the box Paul got in his stocking. How many crayons did Paul's box have?

_____ crayons

_____ x _____ = _____

When my dad bought his TV 20 years ago, it cost $65. The one we just bought cost 10 times more. How much did our new TV cost?

_____ dollars

_____ x _____ = _____

Zippy the Hummingbird flies 25 miles per hour. Freddy the Falcon can fly as fast as 100 mph. How many times faster does Freddy fly than Zippy?

_____ times faster

_____ x _____ = _____

How Many Times?

Directions: Solve the multiplication problems. You may use drawings and equations to show your work.

Our elementary school has 4 buses. The high school has 4 times as many buses. How many buses does the high school have?

_____ buses

_____ x _____ = _____

One sleeve of cookies has 5 cookies inside.   A carton of cookies has 8 times as many cookies as one sleeve. How many cookies are in a carton?

_____ cookies

_____ x _____ = _____

The string of Christmas lights on my door has 18 lightbulbs. My neighbor's door had 4 times as many lights. How many lightbulbs did my neighbor's door have?

_____ lightbulbs

_____ x _____ = _____

This box has 63 pencils. It has 7 times as many pencils as the other box. How many pencils are in the other box?

_____ pencils

_____ x _____ = _____

Andrew had 7¢ in his pocket. His brother, Harold, has 8 times more money than Andrew. How much money does Harold have?

_____ ¢

_____ x _____ = _____

Name: _____

Solving Problems by Estimating

Directions: Solve the problems below. Use mental strategies and estimation with rounding to solve. Choose the best answer.

Starfall Cafe has 763 grams of grape jelly and 542 grams of blueberry jelly. About how many grams of jelly does the Starfall Cafe have?

- ❑ 1300 grams
- ❑ 2700 grams
- ❑ 3500 grams

Zoe bought 45 bags of beads. Each bag had 62 beads. About how many beads did Zoe buy?

- ❑ 3000 beads
- ❑ 2700 beads
- ❑ 100 beads

Deirdre had $478 in her bank account. She bought a new dvd player for $276. About how much money did she have left in her account?

- ❑ $700
- ❑ $200
- ❑ $600

Peter won 848 pounds of spaghetti. He shared his winnings equally with 11 friends. About how much spaghetti did each of the 12 people get?

- ❑ 8 pounds
- ❑ 100 pounds
- ❑ 70 pounds

George filled 13 jars with equal amounts of jellybeans. He started with 742 jellybeans. About how many jellybeans were in each jar?

- ❑ 60 jellybeans
- ❑ 90 jellybeans
- ❑ 145 jellybeans

Name: _____

Solving Problems by Estimating

Directions: Solve the problems below. Show the unknown quantity with a letter. Use mental strategies and estimation with rounding to solve.

Julie and her sisters, Sara and Marney, went dandelion-picking. Julie picked 43 dandelions. Sara picked 26. Marney picked half the amount that Sara picked. How many dandelions did the girls pick?

_____ dandelions (Estimation with rounding)

_____ dandelions (Actual Answer)

The non-fiction shelf at the library had 96 books. Only 37 still remained on the shelf. 4 were found in the fiction section. How many non-fiction books were checked out of the library?

_____ books (Estimation with rounding)

_____ books (Actual Answer)

After collecting cans to recycle, the troop counted their recyclables. Ben had brought in 3 boxes with 6 cans each. Mark collected 4 boxes with 7 bottles each. Jake had 3 boxes with 8 milk jugs each. How many recyclables did the troop collect?

_____ recyclables (Estimation with rounding)

_____ recyclables (Actual Answer)

Our family is traveling across the country.   During the first week we traveled 328 miles. The second week took us 129 miles. During the third week we traveled 53 miles. How many miles did we travel altogether?

_____ miles (Estimation with rounding)

_____ miles (Actual Answer)

Mark had to blow his nose 4 times. Leif had to blow his nose 5 times as many as Mark. Jess had to blow her nose 2 times as many as Mark. How many total times did the three of them blow their noses?

_____ blows (Estimation with rounding)

_____ blows (Actual Answer)

Standard: Math I Operations & Algebraic Thinking I 4.OA.3

©www.CoreCommonStandards.com

Factors and Multiples

Directions: Think about a number's factors, and its multiples. Answer the questions about numbers below.

Which of the following numbers are multiples of 6?	**Which of the following numbers are multiples of 9?**	**Is 7 a prime or composite number?**
❑ 36 ❑ 45 ❑ 18 ❑ 60	❑ 45 ❑ 81 ❑ 18 ❑ 27	_____ **List 7's factors below:**
Is 13 a prime or composite number? _____ **List 13's factors below:**	**Is 8 a prime or composite number?** _____ **List 8's factors below:**	**Which of the following numbers are multiples of 7?** ❑ 23 ❑ 21 ❑ 49 ❑ 63
Is 15 a prime or composite number? _____ **List 15's factors below:**	**Which of the following numbers are multiples of 8?** ❑ 40 ❑ 17 ❑ 24 ❑ 32	**Is 12 a prime or composite number?** _____ **List 12's factors below:**
Which of the following numbers are multiples of 5? ❑ 10 ❑ 25 ❑ 72 ❑ 35	**Is 24 a prime or composite number?** _____ **List 24's factors below:**	**Which of the following numbers are multiples of 12?** ❑ 48 ❑ 13 ❑ 60 ❑ 42

Name: _____

Factors and Multiples

Directions: Think about a number's factors, and its multiples. Answer the questions about numbers below.

Which of the following numbers are multiples of 19?	Which of the following numbers are multiples of 16?	Is 5 a prime or composite number?
❑ 38 ❑ 95 ❑ 20 ❑ 190	❑ 96 ❑ 32 ❑ 81 ❑ 192	_____ List 5's factors below:
Is 14 a prime or composite number? _____ List 14's factors below:	**Is 25 a prime or composite number?** _____ List 25's factors below:	**Which of the following numbers are multiples of 11?** ❑ 44 ❑ 66 ❑ 23 ❑ 76
Is 9 a prime or composite number? _____ List 9's factors below:	**Which of the following numbers are multiples of 20?** ❑ 40 ❑ 80 ❑ 10 ❑ 50	**Is 36 a prime or composite number?** _____ List 36's factors below:
Which of the following numbers are multiples of 25? ❑ 100 ❑ 25 ❑ 60 ❑ 225	**Is 10 a prime or composite number?** _____ List 10's factors below:	**Which of the following numbers are multiples of 10?** ❑ 70 ❑ 45 ❑ 60 ❑ 80

Name: _____

Using Number Patterns

Directions: Look at the figures in a pattern below. Draw the next pattern in each series. Complete the charts to show how the number patterns continues.

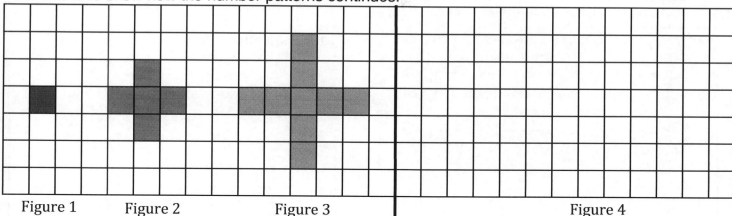

Figure 1   Figure 2   Figure 3   Figure 4

Figure	1	2	3	4	5	6	7
Number of Squares	1	5					
Pattern	--	Add 4					

Figure 1   Figure 2   Figure 3   Figure 4

Figure	1	2	3	4	5	6	7
Number of Squares	4						
Pattern	--						

Complete the patterns below.

a.) 4, 10, 13, 18, 24, 27, 32, 38, 41, _____, _____, _____, _____, _____, _____, _____, _____

b.) 19, 14, 20, 15, 21, 16, 22, _____, _____, _____, _____, _____, _____, _____, _____

c.) 7, 28, 14, 56, 28, 112, 56, _____, _____, _____, _____, _____, _____, _____, _____

Name: _____

Using Number Patterns

Directions: Read the problems below. Think about the pattern rule in each problem.
Use this pattern to help solve the problems.

- -

Crowne Sweet Bakery started the week with 196 cupcakes. On day 1, they had 168 cupcakes left. On day 2, there were only 140 left. If the pattern continues, how many will be left on day 7?

Day	Rule	Cupcakes
0	x - 0	196
1		
2		
3		
4		
5		
6		
7		

Clarise ran 16 laps on Monday, 24 laps on Tuesday, 32 laps on Wednesday. If this pattern continues, how many laps will Clarise run on Friday? What will her total be?

Day	Rule	Laps
M	x + 0	16
T		
W		
Th		
F		
	TOTAL:	

Jake was growing a rose bush. Today there are 2 buds. Each day 3 new buds appeared. How many buds were on the bush after 5 days?

Day	Rule	Buds
0	2 + 3 x 0	2
1	2 + 3 x 1	5
2		
3		
4		
5		

There are 5 pennies in a jar. Each day 4 pennies are added. How many pennies are in the jar after 6 days?

Day	Rule	Pennies
0	5 + 4 x 0	5
1	5 + 4 x 1	
2		
3		
4		
5		
6		

Standard: Math I Operations & Algebraic Thinking I 4.OA.5

©www.CoreCommonStandards.com

Name: _____

How Many Times?

Directions: Read and solve the place value problems below. Think about the value of each place and how it is ten times the value of the place to its right.

1. How much greater is the value of the digit 4 in the hundreds place than the digit 4 in the ones place, in the number 404?	2. How many times greater is the value of the digit in the hundreds place than the value of the digit in the tens place in the number 226?
3. _____ hundreds = 600 ones	4. 9 tens = _____ ones
5. 2 thousands = _____ hundreds	6. _____ ten thousands = 50,000 ones
7. How much greater is the value of the digit 7 in the hundreds place than the digit 7 in the tens place, in the number 772?	8. How many times greater is the value of the digit in the hundreds place than the value of the digit in the ones place in the number 393?
9. 5 thousands = _____ tens	10. 9 hundreds = _____ tens
11. _____ thousands = 40 hundreds	12. 9 ten thousands = _____ ones

Standard: Math I Number & Operations in Base Ten I 4.NBT.1   ©www.CoreCommonStandards.com

Name: _____

Naming Value

Directions: Write the value of each digit in the numbers below.

Write the value of each five.
934,439

9 _____

3 _____

4 _____

4 _____

3 _____

9 _____

Write the value of each digit.
555,555

5 _____

5 _____

5 _____

5 _____

5 _____

5 _____

Write the value of each digit.
66,736

6 _____

6 _____

7 _____

3 _____

6 _____

Write the value of each digit.
454,545

4 _____

5 _____

4 _____

5 _____

4 _____

5 _____

Write the value of each digit.
772,376

7 _____

7 _____

2 _____

3 _____

7 _____

6 _____

Write the value of each two.
2,222,222

2 _____

2 _____

2 _____

2 _____

2 _____

2 _____

2 _____

©www.CoreCommonStandards.com

Name: _____

Knowing Your Place in Place Value

Directions: Read and solve the place value problems below. Think about the value each digit holds when it is in a certain place in a number.

How is the digit 2 in the number 582 different from the digit 2 in the number 528?	What does the digit 5 in the number 587 represent?
The digit 8 in the number 5808 is _____ times greater than the digit 8 in the number 5808. Explain.	57,329 In the number above, which digit has the least value? _____ Explain.
15,246 In the number above, which digit has the greatest value? _____ Explain.	40, 300 In the number above, what is the value of the 4?
Draw a representation of 245.	Draw a representation of 425.
45,6__4 In the number above, the tens place value is 10 times less than the digit in the hundreds place.	Write the number with 9 ones, 5 ten-thousands, 4 hundreds, 6 thousands, and 7 tens.

Name: _____

Knowing Your Place in Place Value

Directions: Read and solve the place value problems below. Think about the value each digit holds when it is in a certain place in a number.

8 + _____ = 18
9 hundreds + _____ tens + 6 ones = 946
5,000 + _____ + 3 + _____ + = 5,973
7,345 = 7 _____ + 5 _____ + 4 _____ + 3 _____
60 + 1 + _____ = 361
_____ + 60 + 5 = 265
circle: 9 H + 3 T + 2 O   <   =   >   8 H + 4 T + 1 O
circle: 5 O + 3 H + 8 O   <   =   >   6 T + 5 O + 2 H
Write this number: four thousand, 6 hundred, three
Which is larger?   24,453   24, 345

Name: _____

Rounding to the Nearest Hundred

Directions: Round the numbers below to the nearest 100. Then, plot the original number on the line.

Round 258 to the nearest 100 = _____. Draw a dot where 258 would be on the number line.

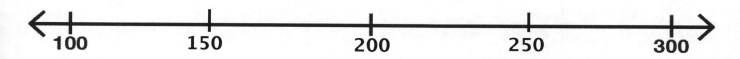

Round 310 to the nearest 100 = _____. Draw a dot where 310 would be on the number line.

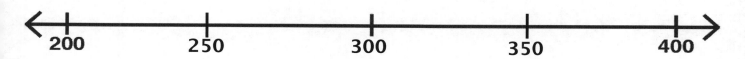

Round 679 to the nearest 100 = _____. Draw a dot where 679 would be on the number line.

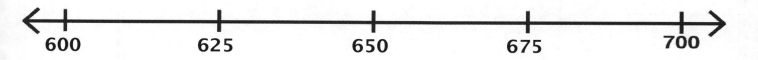

Round 413 to the nearest 100 = _____. Draw a dot where 413 would be on the number line.

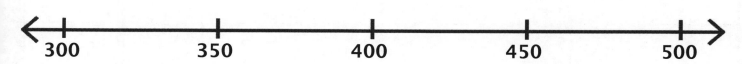

Round 943 to the nearest 100 = _____. Draw a dot where 943 would be on the number line.

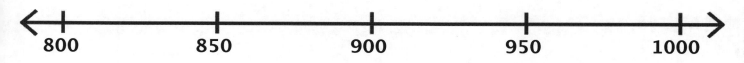

Name: _____

Rounding to the Nearest Whole Number

Directions: Read the numbers below. Round to the nearest hundred, thousand, or ten-thousand.

Round to the nearest hundred...	Round to the nearest thousand...	Round to the nearest ten-thousand...	Round to the nearest hundred...
45,678	78,230	189,345	97,239
_____	_____	_____	_____
Round to the nearest ten-thousand...	Round to the nearest hundred...	Round to the nearest thousand...	Round to the nearest ten-thousand...
28,284	6,239	126,098	345,602
_____	_____	_____	_____
Round to the nearest thousand...	Round to the nearest ten-thousand...	Round to the nearest hundred...	Round to the nearest hundred...
56,994	334,707	4,678	12,445
_____	_____	_____	_____
Round to the nearest thousand...	Round to the nearest hundred...	Round to the nearest thousand...	Round to the nearest ten-thousand...
5,970	12,276	58,034	55,667
_____	_____	_____	_____
Round to the nearest thousand...	Round to the nearest thousand...	Round to the nearest ten-thousand...	Round to the nearest hundred...
34,006	680,135	1,335,998	2,456,914
_____	_____	_____	_____

Level: Fourth Grade   Name: _____

Adding With Fluency

Directions: Solve the addition examples below. Think about the different strategies you have learned to help you solve the equations accurately and quickly.

$$\begin{array}{r} 46 \\ +\ 35 \\ \hline \end{array} \qquad \begin{array}{r} 56 \\ +\ 27 \\ \hline \end{array} \qquad \begin{array}{r} 26 \\ +\ 39 \\ \hline \end{array} \qquad \begin{array}{r} 72 \\ +\ 39 \\ \hline \end{array}$$

$$\begin{array}{r} 65 \\ +\ 18 \\ \hline \end{array} \qquad \begin{array}{r} 65 \\ +\ 49 \\ \hline \end{array} \qquad \begin{array}{r} 88 \\ +\ 24 \\ \hline \end{array} \qquad \begin{array}{r} 52 \\ +\ 75 \\ \hline \end{array}$$

$$\begin{array}{r} 63 \\ +\ 75 \\ \hline \end{array} \qquad \begin{array}{r} 97 \\ +\ 23 \\ \hline \end{array} \qquad \begin{array}{r} 46 \\ +\ 63 \\ \hline \end{array} \qquad \begin{array}{r} 86 \\ +\ 42 \\ \hline \end{array}$$

$$\begin{array}{r} 558 \\ +\ 633 \\ \hline \end{array} \qquad \begin{array}{r} 790 \\ +\ 251 \\ \hline \end{array} \qquad \begin{array}{r} 365 \\ +\ 282 \\ \hline \end{array} \qquad \begin{array}{r} 722 \\ +\ 564 \\ \hline \end{array}$$

$$\begin{array}{r} 5{,}742 \\ +1{,}375 \\ \hline \end{array} \qquad \begin{array}{r} 2{,}585 \\ +1{,}233 \\ \hline \end{array} \qquad \begin{array}{r} 7{,}327 \\ +3{,}486 \\ \hline \end{array} \qquad \begin{array}{r} 4{,}074 \\ +4{,}919 \\ \hline \end{array}$$

Standard: Math I Number & Operations in Base Ten I 4.NBT.4   ©www.CoreCommonStandards.com

Level: Fourth Grade

Name: _____

Subtracting With Fluency

Directions: Solve the subtraction examples below. Think about the different strategies you have learned to help you solve the equations accurately and quickly.

```
   73          83          84          93
-  36       -  47       -  44       -  36
_____     _____     _____     _____


   68          96          68          74
-  27       -  33       -  12       -  33
_____     _____     _____     _____


   88          98          62          94
-  37       -  16       -  49       -  47
_____     _____     _____     _____


  458         736         237         745
- 153       - 465       - 119       - 346
_____     _____     _____     _____


 2,863       2,355       1,843       2,445
-2,246      -1,277      -1,775      -1,338
_____     _____     _____     _____
```

Standard: Math I Number & Operations in Base Ten I 4.NBT.4

©www.CoreCommonStandards.com

118

Name: _____

Multiplying With Two Digits

Directions: Solve the multiplication problems. Use equations, arrays, and/or area models to explain your work.

Farmer Cluck collected 23 dozen eggs.   How many eggs did Farmer Cluck collect.

_____eggs

Joy's dance class had 37 students. Each student held 14 balloons. How many balloons were there in all?

_____ balloons

Mr. Malarkey had an alligator farm. He had 17 alligators. Each alligator laid 22 eggs.

_____alligator eggs

Nana Pinsky grew 11 rosebushes in her garden this year. Each bush bloomed 19 roses. How many roses did Nana grow?

_____ roses

Carl bought 27 bags of Hershey's Kisses for his class. Each bag contained 41 Kisses. How many Kisses were there in all?

_____ Hershey's Kisses

Name: _____

Multiplying Multi-digits

Directions: Solve the multiplication problems. Use equations, arrays, and/or area models to explain your work.

Each day has 1440 minutes. How many minutes are in a week?

_____minutes

Each member of the 5 members of the team donated $2,396 to the charity. How much money in total was donated?

$_____

Shue and his 8 friends each made a tower with blocks.   Each tower had 572 blocks. How many blocks were used altogether?

_____blocks

There are 14,209 dots on each of the 9 pieces of cardboard on the table. How many dots are there in all?

_____ dots

During the parade, Normandy High School Band had 45 members. Each member carried 8 musical scores. How many musical scores did the band carry in all?

_____ musical scores

©www.CoreCommonStandards.com

Name: _____

Division

Directions: Solve the division problems. Think about the relationship between division and multiplication. Use equations, arrays, and/or area models to explain your work.

Paul has 457 peanuts to share with his 8 friends.   How many peanuts will each of the 9 children get? Were there any remaining?

_____ peanuts

_____ remaining peanuts

Claudia collected 1,728 stickers. She divided them equally into 6 different boxes. How many stickers were in each box? Were there any remaining?

_____ stickers

_____ remaining stickers

The 496 students at Gordon School were placed into 8 different teams. How many students were on each team? Were there any remaining?

_____ students

_____ remaining students

Roberto baked 633 slices of pizza. Each of the guests at the party had 4 slices. How many guests were at the party? Were there any slices remaining?

_____ guests

_____ remaining slices

Marney had a box of beads. There were 15,782 beads in her box. She sorted the beads equally into 9 bags. How many beads were in each bag? Were there any remaining?

_____ beads

_____ remaining beads

Name: _____

Division

Directions: Solve the division problems. Think about the relationship between division and multiplication. Draw arrays, and/or area models to explain your work.

$1{,}234 \div 4 =$	$678 \div 3 =$	$243 \div 5 =$
$612 \div 7 =$	$3{,}497 \div 4 =$	$5{,}236 \div 2 =$
$782 \div 8 =$	$6{,}908 \div 9 =$	$2{,}890 \div 5 =$
$2{,}438 \div 3 =$	$553 \div 6 =$	$209 \div 3 =$
$567 \div 5 =$	$628 \div 4 =$	$302 \div 5 =$
$582 \div 9 =$	$528 \div 3 =$	$2{,}742 \div 6 =$
$7{,}459 \div 2 =$	$6{,}268 \div 1 =$	$9{,}653 \div 3 =$

Name: _____

Are They Equivalent?

Directions: Look at the fraction models below. Determine if they show equivalent fractions. Write the fractions below each figure. Write equivalent if the two fractions are equal.

©www.CoreCommonStandards.com

Name: _____

Are They Equivalent?

Directions: Write the proper equivalent fractions into the correct columns.

$\dfrac{1}{2}$	$\dfrac{3}{4}$	$\dfrac{1}{3}$	$\dfrac{1}{5}$

$\dfrac{9}{12}$ $\quad$ $\dfrac{5}{10}$ $\quad$ $\dfrac{4}{6}$ $\quad$ $\dfrac{5}{15}$ $\quad$ $\dfrac{7}{14}$ $\quad$ $\dfrac{2}{10}$ $\quad$ $\dfrac{8}{16}$ $\quad$ $\dfrac{12}{16}$ $\quad$ $\dfrac{5}{25}$

$\dfrac{8}{40}$ $\quad$ $\dfrac{30}{40}$ $\quad$ $\dfrac{9}{27}$ $\quad$ $\dfrac{18}{24}$ $\quad$ $\dfrac{9}{18}$ $\quad$ $\dfrac{10}{30}$ $\quad$ $\dfrac{7}{35}$ $\quad$ $\dfrac{7}{21}$ $\quad$ $\dfrac{27}{36}$

$\dfrac{24}{32}$ $\quad$ $\dfrac{4}{20}$ $\quad$ $\dfrac{11}{33}$ $\quad$ $\dfrac{10}{20}$ $\quad$ $\dfrac{3}{15}$ $\quad$ $\dfrac{21}{28}$ $\quad$ $\dfrac{2}{4}$ $\quad$ $\dfrac{2}{6}$ $\quad$ $\dfrac{3}{9}$

Write as many equivalent fractions you can for: $\dfrac{7}{12}$

Name: _____

Comparing Fractions

Directions: Look at the fractions below. Find the common denominator for both. Write the greater than, less than, or equal to sign to compare the fractions.

$\dfrac{3}{6}$ $\boxed{<}$ $\dfrac{5}{8}$ $\dfrac{12}{24}$ $\dfrac{15}{24}$	$\dfrac{7}{9}$ $\Box$ $\dfrac{2}{8}$	$\dfrac{1}{6}$ $\Box$ $\dfrac{3}{7}$	$\dfrac{2}{9}$ $\Box$ $\dfrac{3}{7}$
$\dfrac{4}{7}$ $\Box$ $\dfrac{5}{6}$	$\dfrac{4}{9}$ $\Box$ $\dfrac{3}{8}$	$\dfrac{8}{9}$ $\Box$ $\dfrac{3}{5}$	$\dfrac{7}{8}$ $\Box$ $\dfrac{2}{6}$
$\dfrac{6}{9}$ $\Box$ $\dfrac{5}{7}$	$\dfrac{6}{8}$ $\Box$ $\dfrac{2}{9}$	$\dfrac{6}{7}$ $\Box$ $\dfrac{4}{9}$	$\dfrac{4}{8}$ $\Box$ $\dfrac{3}{5}$
$\dfrac{4}{6}$ $\Box$ $\dfrac{3}{7}$	$\dfrac{2}{3}$ $\Box$ $\dfrac{4}{7}$	$\dfrac{2}{9}$ $\Box$ $\dfrac{2}{3}$	$\dfrac{1}{6}$ $\Box$ $\dfrac{6}{9}$
$\dfrac{7}{10}$ $\Box$ $\dfrac{2}{13}$	$\dfrac{4}{12}$ $\Box$ $\dfrac{3}{9}$	$\dfrac{5}{12}$ $\Box$ $\dfrac{6}{7}$	$\dfrac{1}{8}$ $\Box$ $\dfrac{2}{7}$
$\dfrac{4}{7}$ $\Box$ $\dfrac{8}{9}$	$\dfrac{5}{15}$ $\Box$ $\dfrac{7}{12}$	$\dfrac{6}{14}$ $\Box$ $\dfrac{7}{10}$	$\dfrac{5}{12}$ $\Box$ $\dfrac{6}{18}$

Level: Fourth Grade   Name: _____

More? Less? Equal?

Directions: Look at the fraction models below. Write the fraction each model represents. Convert the fractions to common denominators to determine which is greater, less, or if they are equal.

Standard: Math I Number & Operations-Fractions I 4.NF.2

©www.CoreCommonStandards.com

Name: _____

Comparing Fraction Models

Directions: Look at the fraction models below. Write the fraction each model represents. Convert the fractions to common denominators to determine which is greater, less, or if they are equal.

1.

_____ ☐ _____

2.

_____ ☐ _____

3.

_____ ☐ _____

4.

_____ ☐ _____

5.

_____ ☐ _____

6.

_____ ☐ _____

7.

_____ ☐ _____

8.

_____ ☐ _____

Name: _____

Adding Fractions

Directions: Solve the fraction addition equations below. Draw fraction models or use the fraction bars to help.

$1/4 + 2/4 =$	$2/6 + 3/6 =$
$3/8 + 4/8 =$	$1/16 + 9/16 =$
$4/6 + 2/6 =$	$2/3 + 1/3 =$
$1/5 + 3/5 =$	$2/8 + 4/8 =$
$3\ 1/4 + 2\ 3/4 =$	$4\ 1/8 + 4/8 =$
$8\ 5/16 + 2\ 3/16 =$	$7\ 2/5 + 2/5 =$
$2\ 2/8 + 4\ 2/8 =$	$8\ 3/6 + 4\ 2/6 =$

Standard: Math I Number & Operations-Fractions I 4.NF.3

©www.CoreCommonStandards.com

Fraction Bars

1																

| 1/2 |||||||| 1/2 ||||||||

| 1/3 ||||| 1/3 ||||| 1/3 |||||

| 1/4 |||| 1/4 |||| 1/4 |||| 1/4 ||||

| 1/5 ||| 1/5 ||| 1/5 ||| 1/5 ||| 1/5 ||| 1/5 |||

| 1/8 || 1/8 || 1/8 || 1/8 || 1/8 || 1/8 || 1/8 || 1/8 ||

| 1/16 | 1/16 | 1/16 | 1/16 | 1/16 | 1/16 | 1/16 | 1/16 | 1/16 | 1/16 | 1/16 | 1/16 | 1/16 | 1/16 | 1/16 | 1/16 |

Name: _____

Decomposing Fractions

Directions: Look at the fractions below. Decompose the fractions into smaller parts. Draw a diagram to show your thinking.

4/6	6/8
4/6 = 1/6 + 1/6 + 1/6 + 1/6 or 4/6 = 1/6 + 3/6 or 4/6 = 2/6 + 2/6	
5/12	**7/10**
3/9	**4/12**
6/15	**8/20**

©www.CoreCommonStandards.com

Name: _____

Multiply Fractions by a Whole Number

Directions: Solve the fraction multiplication examples below. Use the strategy illustrated in the example.

Example: **4 x 2/5** can be looked at as **8 x 1/5** which would be **8/5**. Reduced, this fraction is **1 3/5**. So, **4 x 2/5 = 1 3/5**	**2 x 3/7 =**	**4/15 x 7**
4 x 8/14	**6 x 4/6**	**4/7 x 3**
9/10 x 3	**6/7 x 5**	**5/6 x 2**
3/8 x 5	**4 x 3/9**	**2/8 x 8**

Standard: Math I Number & Operations-Fractions I 4.NF.4

©www.CoreCommonStandards.com

Level: Fourth Grade   Name: _____

Solving Problems with Fractions

Directions: Solve the fraction stories below.

In the last race, Peter ran 8 laps around the track. Kyle ran 1/4 as many laps as Peter. How many laps did Kyle run?	The seals at Mystic Aquarium are fed 6 buckets of fish each day. The walruses are fed 4/6 as much as the seals. How much are the walruses fed?
George picked 9 roses. Drew picked 1/3 as many roses as George. How many roses did Drew pick?	Francine had 12 votes for Class President. Arthur had 2/3 as many votes as Francine. How many votes did Arthur get?
Janet and her brother picked 7 bushels of apples on Sunday. Mom used 1/3 of the bushels to bake pies. How many bushels of apples did mom use?	We made cookies for our class. The recipe called for 5/8 a cup of sugar. We made 4 batches of cookies. How many cups of sugar did we need?
**In March, we received 16 inches rain. In April, the total rainfall was 1/4 less inches. How many inches did it rain in April?	**Susan has 12 stickers. Her friend Fran has 2/3 more stickers than Susan. How many stickers does Fran have?

Standard: Math I Number & Operations-Fractions I 4.NF.4   ©www.CoreCommonStandards.com
132

Name: _____

Adding Fractions with Denominators of 10 and 100

Directions: Write the equivalent fraction with the denominator of 100 for the fraction with a denominator of 10. Then add the two fractions together.

Example $\frac{4}{10} + \frac{7}{100}$	$\frac{6}{10} + \frac{8}{100}$	$\frac{3}{10} + \frac{9}{100}$
$\frac{4}{10} = \frac{40}{100}$ SO…	$\frac{6}{10} = \frac{}{100}$	$\frac{3}{10} = \frac{}{100}$
$\frac{40}{100} + \frac{7}{100} = \frac{47}{}$	$\frac{60}{100} + \frac{8}{100} =$	$\frac{30}{100} + \frac{9}{100} =$
$\frac{7}{10} + \frac{9}{100}$	$\frac{1}{10} + \frac{3}{100}$	$\frac{9}{10} + \frac{2}{100}$
$\frac{7}{10} = \frac{}{100}$	$\frac{1}{10} = \frac{}{100}$	$\frac{9}{10} = \frac{}{100}$
$\frac{7}{100} + \frac{9}{100} =$	$\frac{10}{100} + \frac{3}{100} =$	$\frac{}{100} + \frac{}{100} =$
$\frac{4}{10} + \frac{5}{100}$	$\frac{5}{10} + \frac{8}{100}$	$\frac{9}{10} + \frac{4}{100}$
$\frac{4}{10} = \frac{}{100}$	$\frac{5}{10} = \frac{}{100}$	$\frac{9}{10} = \frac{}{100}$
$\frac{}{100} + \frac{}{100} =$	$\frac{}{100} + \frac{}{100} =$	$\frac{}{100} + \frac{}{100} =$
$\frac{6}{10} + \frac{6}{100}$	$\frac{3}{10} + \frac{7}{100}$	$\frac{6}{10} + \frac{1}{100}$
$\frac{6}{10} = \frac{}{100}$	$\frac{3}{10} = \frac{}{100}$	$\frac{6}{10} = \frac{}{100}$
$\frac{}{100} + \frac{}{100} =$	$\frac{}{100} + \frac{}{100} =$	$\frac{}{100} + \frac{}{100} =$
$\frac{5}{10} + \frac{7}{100}$	$\frac{2}{10} + \frac{2}{100}$	$\frac{8}{10} + \frac{6}{100}$
$\frac{5}{10} = \frac{}{100}$	$\frac{2}{10} = \frac{}{100}$	$\frac{8}{10} = \frac{}{100}$
$\frac{}{100} + \frac{}{100} =$	$\frac{}{100} + \frac{}{100} =$	$\frac{}{100} + \frac{}{100} =$

Level: Fourth Grade   Name: _____

Adding Fractions with Denominators of 10 and 100

Directions: Add the fractions. Notice the denominators are not the same.

$3/10 = 30/100$ so... $3/10 + 4/100 = 34/100$	1. $\dfrac{5}{10} + \dfrac{8}{100} =$	2. $\dfrac{2}{10} + \dfrac{9}{100} =$
3. $\dfrac{1}{10} + \dfrac{5}{100} =$	4. $\dfrac{3}{10} + \dfrac{8}{100} =$	5. $\dfrac{8}{10} + \dfrac{2}{100} =$
6. $\dfrac{4}{10} + \dfrac{4}{100} =$	7. $\dfrac{7}{10} + \dfrac{1}{100} =$	8. $\dfrac{9}{10} + \dfrac{5}{100} =$
9. $\dfrac{7}{10} + \dfrac{3}{100} =$	10. $\dfrac{8}{10} + \dfrac{3}{100} =$	11. $\dfrac{9}{10} + \dfrac{2}{100} =$
12. $\dfrac{7}{10} + \dfrac{5}{100} =$	13. $\dfrac{4}{10} + \dfrac{6}{100} =$	14. $\dfrac{6}{10} + \dfrac{3}{100} =$
15. $\dfrac{9}{10} + \dfrac{8}{100} =$	16. $\dfrac{2}{10} + \dfrac{7}{100} =$	17. $\dfrac{5}{10} + \dfrac{5}{100} =$
18. $\dfrac{8}{10} + \dfrac{7}{100} =$	19. $\dfrac{9}{10} + \dfrac{7}{100} =$	20. $\dfrac{4}{10} + \dfrac{8}{100} =$
21. $\dfrac{3}{10} + \dfrac{2}{100} =$	22. $\dfrac{2}{10} + \dfrac{6}{100} =$	23. $\dfrac{8}{10} + \dfrac{1}{100} =$

©www.CoreCommonStandards.com

Name: _____

Modeling with Fractions and Decimals

Directions: Write the decimals and fractions represented by the grids. Then, fill in the grids to show the given fraction or decimals. Write the second form.

Write a fraction and decimal for the model.	Write a fraction and decimal for the model.	Write a fraction and decimal for the model.
_____ _____ 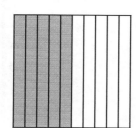	_____ _____ 	_____ _____ 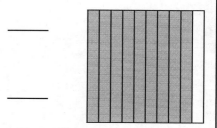
Write a fraction and decimal for the model.	Write a fraction and decimal for the model.	Write a fraction and decimal for the model.
_____ _____ 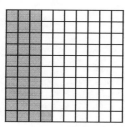	_____ _____ 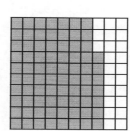	_____ _____ 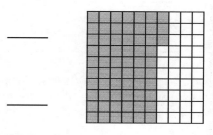
Draw a model to show the fraction. Write the fraction as a decimal. $\dfrac{7}{10}$ 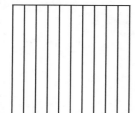 _____	Draw a model to show the decimal. Write the decimal as a fraction. 0.6 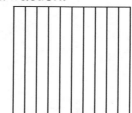 _____	Draw a model to show the decimal. Write the decimal as a fraction. 0.4 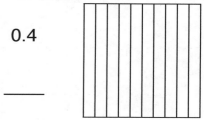 _____
Draw a model to show the decimal. Write the decimal as a fraction. 0.71 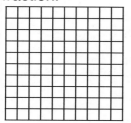 _____	Draw a model to show the fraction. Write the fraction as a decimal. $\dfrac{65}{100}$ 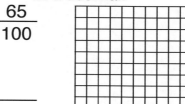 _____	Draw a model to show the decimal. Write the decimal as a fraction. 0.29 _____

Name: _____

Finding the Right Place on the Number Line

Directions: Fill in the blanks with the correct decimal numbers.

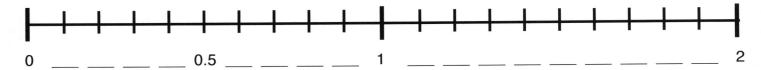

0 ___ ___ ___ ___ 0.5 ___ ___ ___ ___ 1 ___ ___ ___ ___ ___ ___ ___ ___ ___ 2

tenths

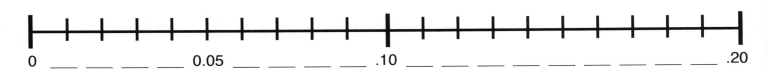

0 ___ ___ ___ ___ 0.05 ___ ___ ___ ___ .10 ___ ___ ___ ___ ___ ___ ___ ___ ___ .20

hundredths

Decimals The Robot is calling out decimals. Draw dots in the correct position for the decimals on the number line below.

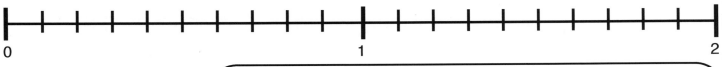

0   1   2

.34   .7   .4   .75

1.43   1.7   1.39

.82   .25   1.9

1.2   .57   1.36

©www.CoreCommonStandards.com

Name: _____

Comparing Decimals to Hundredths

Directions: Round the decimals to the nearest *__hundredths__* place. Write the proper symbol, **<, =,** or **>**, between the two decimals in each example.

.347 ↓ .350 〇 .458 ↓ .460	.317 〇 .384	.277 〇 .239
.366 〇 .365	.847 〇 .899	.529 〇 .581
.667 〇 .662	.170 〇 .107	.329 〇 .635
.992 〇 .915	.899 〇 .900	.329 〇 .372
.554 〇 .520	.293 〇 .392	.290 〇 .301
.200 〇 .199	.527 〇 .552	.854 〇 .890

Standard: Math I Number & Operations-Fractions I 4.NF.7

©www.CoreCommonStandards.com

Name: _____

Ordering Decimals to Hundredths

Directions: Round the numbers to the nearest hundredth. Order the new decimals according to the directions. Use a chart like the one at the right if you need help.

ones	.	tenths	hundredths	thousandths

Order greatest to least.

7.99   7.90   7.92   7.82   7.84   7.74

_____ _____ _____ _____ _____ _____

Order greatest to least.

5.45   5.72   5.61   4.98   4.12   4.01

_____ _____ _____ _____ _____ _____

Order greatest to least.

9.000   9.456   9.003   9.078   9.336   9.112

_____ _____ _____ _____ _____ _____

Order greatest to least.

3.01   3.14   3.71   3.21   3.56   2.99

_____ _____ _____ _____ _____ _____

Order least to greatest.

6.26   6.79   6.91   6.52   6.62   6.33

_____ _____ _____ _____ _____ _____

Order least to greatest.

1.200   1.998   1.456   1.300   1.356   1.970

_____ _____ _____ _____ _____ _____

Order least to greatest.

4.20   4.99   5.12   3.23   3.71   4.04

_____ _____ _____ _____ _____ _____

Order least to greatest.

1.99   2.22   .880   1.03   2.30   .723

_____ _____ _____ _____ _____ _____

Standard: Math I Number & Operations-Fractions I 4.NF.7

Level: Fourth Grade

Name: _____

Know Your Measurements

Directions: Complete the Measurement Conversion Tables below. Then, list the number pairs to match.

meters	centimeters
1	
2	
3	

(__ , __)   (__ , __)   (__ , __)

kilograms	grams
1	
2	
3	

(__ , __)   (__ , __)   (__ , __)

pounds	ounces
1	
2	
3	

(__ , __)   (__ , __)   (__ , __)

liters	milliliters
1	
2	
3	

(__ , __)   (__ , __)   (__ , __)

minutes	seconds
1	
2	
3	

(__ , __)   (__ , __)   (__ , __)

Standard: Math I Measurement & Data I 4.MD.1

©www.CoreCommonStandards.com

139

Name: _____

Time to Convert!

Directions: Complete the Conversion Tables. Rules are in **BOLD** to help show how to convert.

METRIC MASS

Kilograms	Grams	Milligrams
1 kg = 1,000,000 mg	**1 kg = 1000 g**	**1000 mg = 1 g**
_____ g = 2 kg	50 g = _____ mg	_____ mg = 3 g
2,000 g = _____ kg	3 g = _____ mg	5000 mg = _____ g
8 kg = _____ g	4000 g = _____ kg	2 kg = _____ mg

METRIC LENGTH

Kilometer	Meter	Centimeter	Millimeter
1 km = 1000 m **1 km = 1,000,000 mm**	**1 m = 100 cm** **1 m = 1000 mm**	**100 cm = 1 m** **100,000 cm = 1 km**	**1000 mm = 1 m** **10 mm = 1 cm**
1 km = _____ m	3 m = _____ cm	10 cm = _____ mm	50 mm = _____ cm
3 km = _____ m	4 m = _____ mm	500 cm = _____ m	8000 mm = _____ m
2 km = _____ mm	5000 m = _____ km	9000 cm = _____ m	90 mm = _____ cm

CUSTOMARY LENGTH

Mile	Yard	Foot	Inch
1 mi = 5280 ft **1 mi = 1760 yd**	**1 yd = 3 ft** **1 yd = 36 in**	**1 ft = 1/3 yard** **1 ft = 12 in**	**1 in = 1/12 ft** **1 in = 1/36 yd**
3 mi = _____ ft	12 yd = _____ ft	18 ft = _____ yd	72 in = _____ yd
2 mi = _____ yd	6 yd = _____ in	6 ft = _____ in	24 in = _____ ft
5 mi = _____ ft	2 yd = _____ ft	9 ft = _____ in	48 in = _____ ft

Standard: Math l Measurement & Data l 4.MD.1

©www.CoreCommonStandards.com

Name: _____

Solving Problems I

Directions: Solve the problems below. Think about what operation you need to use.

Add the money amounts. $14.90 $236.81 36.82 346.98 44.27 32.58 + 17.02 + 40.01	Sarah and Julie began filling their water balloons at 5:12 pm. Their water balloon fight lasted 40 minutes. It took them 15 minutes to clean up all of the broken balloons. What time did the two friends finish their game and clean-up?

Solve:
 	
 a.   3 ft 2 in + 6 ft 11 in = _____ ft _____ in
 	
 b.   6 hrs 30 min
      +   3 hrs 35 min
 	
       ____hrs ____min
 	
 c.   5 lbs 6 oz + 6 lbs 8 oz = _____ lbs _____ oz
	The toy store sells a pack of 3 tops for $2.34. How much does each top cost?

Subtract the money amounts. $235.87 $1,983.55 - 197.34 - 486.88 $354,912.09 $1,223,542.00 - 120,374.33 - 1,098,335.09	**Which is the better buy?** ☐ 2-pack pen set for $0.80 ☐ 3-pack pencil set for $1.23 Show your work.

Name: _____

Solving Problems II

Directions: Solve the problems below. Think about what operation you need to use.

In mom's silverware drawer, there are 9 spoons. There are 7 more knives than spoons, and twice as many forks as spoons. How many pieces of silverware does mom have in her drawer?

Sheila gave her daughter, Patricia, $65.00 to buy new school clothes. She spent $10 on a t-shirt, $14 on a skirt, $12 on leggings, and $22 on a jacket. How much money did Patricia have left?

At Zulu's Bike Shop there are 14 bicycles, 22 tricycles, and 3 unicycles. How many wheels are there on all the cycles at the bike shop?

Frankie's Bakery had 34 donuts, 17 cupcakes, 24 danish, and 20 cream puffs. Bob bought all of them and shared them with 4 of his friends. How many treats did each person get?
(Hint: There are 5 people, not 4!!!)

Name: _____

Finding Perimeter and Area

Directions: Read and solve the perimeter and area problems below

Patricia's mom wanted a new rug that would fit her bedroom. The room is a rectangular. One wall is 13 feet. Another is 10 feet.

What is the perimeter of the room?

What is the area?

Kyle made a triangle with his blocks. It was an equilateral triangle. He measured one side and the length was 15 cm. **What is the perimeter of Kyle's triangle?**

Grandpa wanted to put up a fence around his garden. The garden had 6 sides, but was not a regular hexagon. He measured five sides and the measurements were 10 ft, 4 ft, 12 ft, 8 ft, and 6 ft. The total perimeter was 45 feet. **What was the measurement of the 6th side?**

Drew painted a wall in his room. The wall is a square with one side measuring 96 inches.

What is the perimeter of the wall?

What is the area of the wall?

The new school media room needs new carpeting. The room is 4 yards by 7 yards. Carpet costs $45 per square yard. **How much will it cost to buy new carpet for the media room?**

Mom bought a new border for my bedroom. The border will go around the room on each wall. My room is a rectangle with one wall measuring 7 feet and another wall measuring 6 feet. The border costs $2 per foot. **How much money did mom spend on the border for my room?**

Name: _____

Finding Perimeter and Area

Directions: Solve the perimeter and area problems below.

The area of the rectangle below is $70cm^2$, and it's width is 10cm.

What is the length, *l*, of the rectangle?

10 cm

l

The length of *l* is _____

What is the perimeter of the Pentagon in Virginia if its sides are each 921 feet long?

The perimeter is _____.

The length of the rectangle is twice the length of the width. What is the rectangle's area?

17mm

The area is _____.

What is the width of a rectangle with a length of 6 inches and a perimeter of 22?

The width is _____.

What is the length of a rectangle with a width of 7cm and an area of $21cm^2$?

The length is _____.

Find the perimeter of this shape.
The perimeter is _____.

15 cm

2 cm

10 cm

4 cm

4 cm

4 cm

4 cm

6 cm

8 cm

7 cm

Level: Fourth Grade   Name: _____

Line Plots

Directions: Use the line plots below to answer the questions.

This line plot depicts the number of different weight candy bars sold by the third grade. Each X stands for 5 children.

```
X
X
X
X          X                    X
X          X                    X
X          X          X         X
X          X          X         X
X          X          X         X
_____
1/4 lb    1/2 lb    3/4 lb    1 lb
         Weight of Candy Bars
```

This line plot depicts the size of four different kinds of insect eggs collected by Trevor and Tyrone. Each X stands for 2 eggs.

```
                                    X
X                                   X
X                                   X
X          X                        X
X          X              X         X
_____
2/10 cm    1/2 cm    6/10 cm    9/10 cm
butterfly  grasshopper horned    praying
                      beetle     mantis
          Size of insect eggs.
```

Answer the questions using the line plot above.

1. How many total children sold candy bars?

2. How many children sold candy bars larger than 1/2 pound?

3. How many more children sold 1/2 lb candy bars than 3/4 lb candy bars?

4. *What percentage of the total amount of candy bars sold were 1 lb?

Answer the questions using the line plot above.

1. How many total eggs were found?

2. How many times bigger is the horned beetle egg than the butterfly egg?

3. How many more praying mantis eggs were found than grasshopper eggs?

4. *What percentage of the total amount of eggs found were 1/2 cm in size?

Standard: Math I Measurement & Data I 4.MD.4   ©www.CoreCommonStandards.com

145

Level: Fourth Grade

Name: _____

Making Line Plots

Directions: Use the data from each problem to create a line plot.

Brendan and his sister, Chloe, have an insect collection. They measured the lengths of all of their insects . Use their data to construct a line plot for the insects' lengths.

4 insects are 1/6 inch long.
6 insects are 1/2 inch long.
2 insects are 1 inch long.
5 insects are 1/8 inch long.
3 insects are 1/3 inch long.

_____

Ask a question using the data from your line plot.

Drew has a bag of legos. He sorted his legos into different lengths. Use Drew's data to create a line plot for the legos' lengths.

13 legos are 32 mm long.
15 legos are 8 mm long.
19 legos are 48 mm long.
10 legos are 16 mm long.
9 legos are 24 mm long.
4 legos are 64 mm long.

_____

Ask a question using the data from your line plot.

Standard: Math I Measurement & Data I 4.MD.4

©www.CoreCommonStandards.com

Name: _____

Turns and Degrees

Directions: Look at the angles below. Choose the proper degree or fraction-of-a-turn for each.

What fraction of a turn is this angle ?  ☐ 1/4 of a turn ☐ 1/2 of a turn ☐ 3/4 of a turn ☐ 1 full turn	What fraction of a turn is this angle ? ☐ 3/4 of a turn ☐ 1/2 of a turn ☐ 1/4 of a turn ☐ 1 full turn	What is the measurement of this angle? 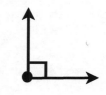 ☐ 45° ☐ 270° ☐ 90° ☐ 180°
What is the measurement of this angle? ☐ 90° ☐ 180° ☐ -90° ☐ 270°	What fraction of a turn is this angle ? 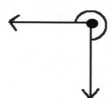 ☐ 1/4 of a turn ☐ 1/2 of a turn ☐ 3/4 of a turn ☐ 1 full turn	What degree of a turn is this angle ? 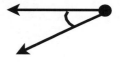 ☐ less than 90° ☐ more than 90° ☐ more than 180° ☐ 1 full turn
What fraction of a turn is this angle ? 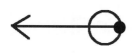 ☐ 1/4 of a turn ☐ 1/2 of a turn ☐ 3/4 of a turn ☐ 1 full turn	What is the measurement of this angle?  ☐ 90° ☐ less than 90° ☐ between 90° and 180° ☐ more than 180°	What is the measurement of this angle?  ☐ 360° ☐ 270° ☐ 90° ☐ 180°

More Turns and Degrees

Directions: Draw angles below that follow the criteria.

Draw an angle that shows a 1/4 turn.	Draw an angle with less than 90˚.
Draw an angle between 90˚ and 180˚	Draw an angle that shows a 3/4 turn.
Draw an angle that shows a 1/2 turn.	Draw an angle over 180˚

Name: _____

Drawing Angles

Directions: Use a protractor to draw an angle having the measurement shown for each example. Write whether the angle is *acute, right, obtuse,* or *straight.*

45°	120°	35°
_____	_____	_____
179°	150°	80°
_____	_____	_____
90°	22°	75°
_____	_____	_____
24°	110°	180°
_____	_____	_____

Name: _____

Measure the Angles

Directions: Use a protractor to measure the angles shown for each example. Write whether the angle is *acute, right, obtuse,* or *straight.*

©www.CoreCommonStandards.com

Name: _____

Measure the Angles

Directions: Find the measurement of each unknown complimentary and supplementary angle.

What is the measurement of ∠ IGF? 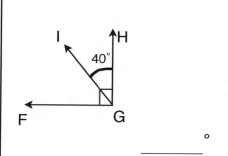 _____°	What is the measurement of ∠ ABC? 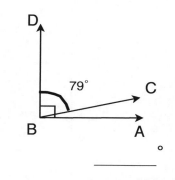 _____°	What is the measurement of ∠ XYZ? 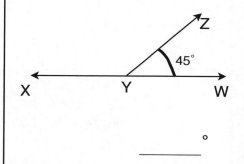 _____°
What is the measurement of ∠ PIG? 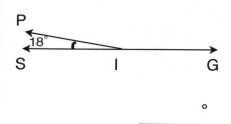 _____°	What is the measurement of ∠ ANT? 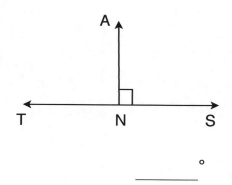 _____°	What is the measurement of ∠ NMO? 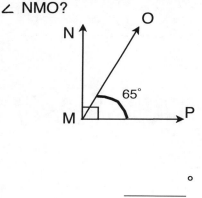 _____°
What is the measurement of ∠ LIP? 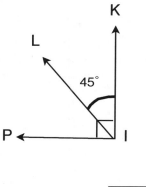 _____°	What is the measurement of ∠ RED? 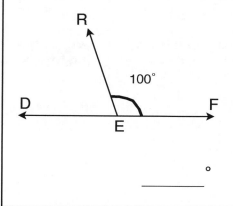 _____°	What is the measurement of ∠ MOP? 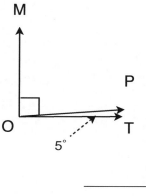 _____°

Name: _____

Solving Problems with Angles

Directions: Solve the problems below. Think about what operation you need to use.

What do we have? An 85° angle with two parts, one being 55°. What is the unknown angle? ° _____	**What do we have?** A straight angle with three parts. One part is 43°. Another part is 10° more. What is the missing angle's degree? ° _____
What do we have? A right angle split into halves. How many degrees is each half? ° _____	**What do we have?** Three non-overlapping angles, 45°, 67°, and 22°. What is the measure of the total angle? ° _____
What do we have? One angle of 180° is split into three equal parts. What is the measure of each part's angle? ° _____	**What do we have?** A reflex angle measuring 225° is split into 2 parts, one being 170°. What is the measure of the second angle? ° _____
What do we have? A straight angle is split into 3 non-equal parts. Write three possible combinations of degrees for each of the angles. 1. ____° ____° ____° = 180° 2. ____° ____° ____° = 180° 3. ____° ____° ____° = 180°	**What do we have?** A 90° angle with two parts, one measuring 1/3 of the total measure. What is the measure of the second angle? ° _____

Name: _____

Drawing Lines and Angles

Directions: Draw the following lines and angles. Use a ruler.

Draw line segments: $\overline{AH}$	$\overline{CK}$	$\overline{BL}$
Draw angles: ∠ HOP	∠ ACT	∠ PAN
Draw parallel lines: $\overleftrightarrow{MN} \parallel \overleftrightarrow{CP}$	$\overleftrightarrow{RF} \parallel \overleftrightarrow{SB}$	$\overleftrightarrow{DK} \parallel \overleftrightarrow{YZ}$
Draw perpendicular lines: $\overleftrightarrow{RG} \perp \overleftrightarrow{SM}$	$\overleftrightarrow{FW} \perp \overleftrightarrow{PL}$	$\overleftrightarrow{YH} \perp \overleftrightarrow{OK}$

Standard: Math I Geometry I 4.G.1

©www.CoreCommonStandards.com

Name: _____

Identify Properties of Shapes

Directions: Find the following properties of each shape shown.

Locate and label the parallel lines. ‖

 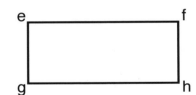 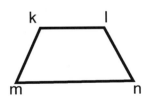 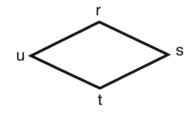

Locate and label the line segments. ▬

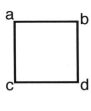 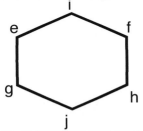 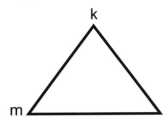 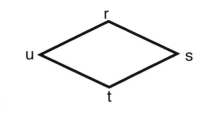

Locate and label the right angles. ⌐

 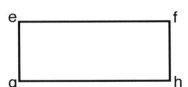 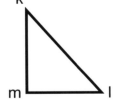 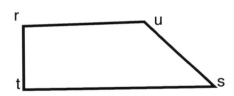

Locate and label the acute angles. (

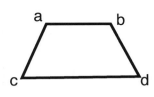 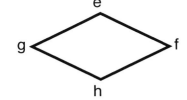 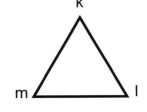 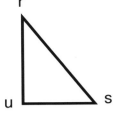

Locate and label the obtuse angles. (

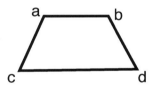 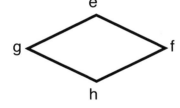 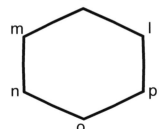 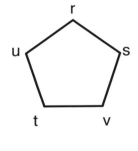

Standard: Math I Geometry I 4.G.1

Name: _____

Classifying Two-Dimensional Figures

Directions: Draw the shapes into the boxes that best describe their attributes.

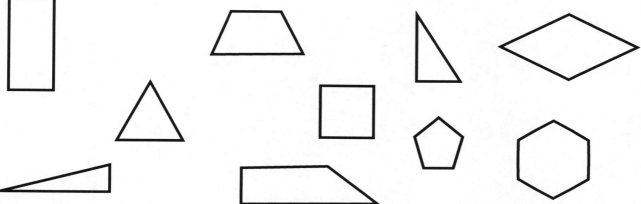

Right Angles Only	One Set of Parallel Lines
Contains At Least 2 Acute Angles	**Right Triangles**
More Than One Set of Parallel Lines	**Triangles**

Name: _____

Classifying Two-Dimensional Figures

Directions: Use the venn diagram below to classify 2-D shapes that follow the rules given.

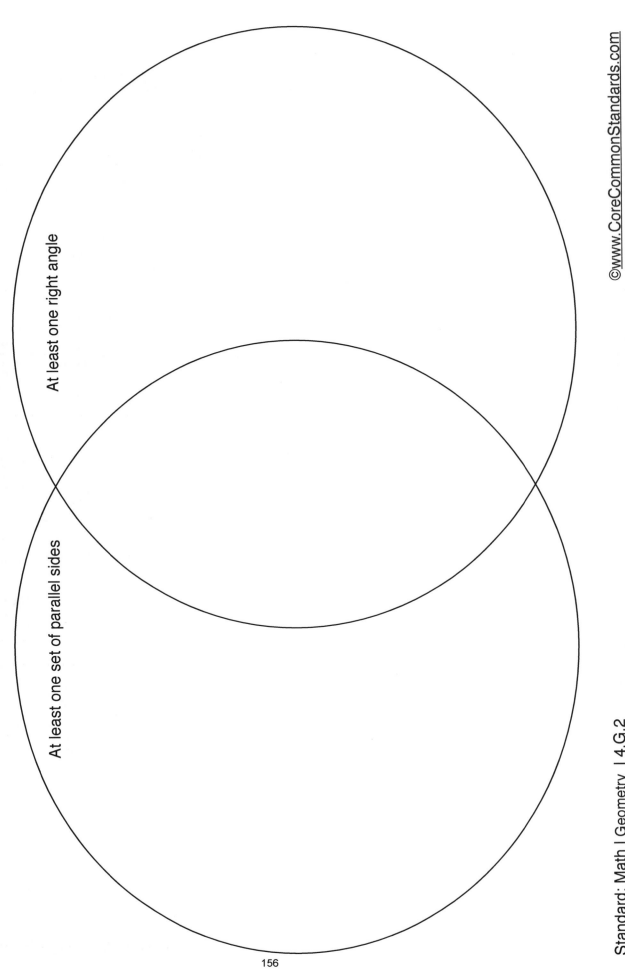

At least one right angle

At least one set of parallel sides

Level: Fourth Grade

Standard: Math I Geometry I 4.G.2

Name: _____

Identifying Symmetrical Shapes

Directions: Write Yes if the shape is symmetrical or No if it is not. Then, draw all lines of symmetry.

a.

_____

b.

_____

c.

_____

d.

_____

e.

_____

f.

_____

g.

_____

h.

_____

i.

_____

Standard: Math I Geometry I 4.G.3

©www.CoreCommonStandards.com

Level: Fourth Grade

Name: _____

Finding Symmetry

Directions: Draw all correct lines of symmetry for each shape.
Complete the symmetrical shapes.

a.

b.

c.

d.

e.

f.

g.

h.

i.

Standard: Math I Geometry I 4.G.3

158

©www.CoreCommonStandards.com

Common Core State Standards
Educating classrooms one standard at a time.

Made in the USA
San Bernardino, CA
28 March 2016